Memoirs of a Royal Lover

Memoirs of a Royal Lover

Dontae Cottrell

Published by CLF PUBLISHING, LLC. 3281 Guasti Road, Seventh Floor, Ontario, CA 91761.
(760) 669-8149.

Copyright © 2013 by Dontae Cottrell. All rights reserved. No portion of this book may be reproduced, stored in a retrieval system, or transmitted by any form or any means electronically, photocopied, recorded, or any other except for brief quotations in printed reviews, without the prior permission of the publisher.

Cover Design by Senir Design. Contact information- info@senirdesign.com.

ISBN # 978-0-9892358-1-5

Printed in the United States of America.

Table of Contents

I Can't Resist	9
Be with You	10
Loved in my Kitchen	11
King's Love	13
My Dream Girl	15
You're a Love Freak	16
Everlasting	18
My World	20
Unbelievable	22
Deep Dreaming	24
Thoughts of You	25
Royal Room	27
Body to Body	29
Enter Your Love	31
Dream Catcher	33
Another's Man Girl	35
The Experience of a Queen	37
My Magic Love Show	39
In Due Time, You will be Mine	41
My Throne	42
Office Love	44
Formal Invite	46
I Can't Explain Your Love	49
Loving You to the Tenth Power	50
Just You and Me	51
My Masterpiece	52
True Love	54
A Brand New Day	55
Counting Down the Days	56
Imagine	57
My Twelve Royal Ways	58
One Night	61
My Undying Love	63

Lost Love	65
Take My Time	67
Up All Night	69
Pleasure	71
Falling in Love	73
Beyond the Clouds	74
Never Ending	75
A Love Groove Called You	76
All I Ever Wanted	77
Drunken Night	78
My Mind Screaming Out	79
Come See Me	80
My Player Bone is Gone	82
Rejection	83
Borrowed Time	85
Our Love	87
Without You	88
My Beautiful Find	90
All Alone	91
Deep Inside	93
Just to See You Again	95
Wanting You	96
Love Power	98
The Big Day	99
Motionless	103
Remember that Time	104
Familiar Love	106
It's All about You	108
I Surrender	110
Under the Sun	113
My Roller Coaster Ride	115
A Fool in Love	117
My Back Bone	119
Endless Love	121
Hold You Down	122
My Rib	124

My Gift	126
My Love Planet	128
My Girl Bad	131
Promise Land	133
The First Time	135
My Love Slave	138
A Feeling You Never Felt Before	142
Rain Drops	144
She Isn't You	148
When Your Love Calls	150
Exploring Your Body	154
Unforgettable Night	156
The Essence of This Woman	158
Love Where Are You	160
Break You Down	161
A Lifetime	163
Never Ending Love	164
My Spanish Rose	166
Never Duplicated	169
Lovers' Land	171
Unbreakable	174
Blow Your Mind	175
He's Where You Are...	177
My Computer Love	178
Pleasing You	179
My Life Commitment	180
One and Only	181
My Vows	182
Perfect in my Eyes	183
Showdown	184
Definition of Love	186
Co-Star	188
Because of You	191
In the Middle of Your Love	192
Honest Love	194
Love in the Shower	196

The Key to My Love	198
Can I Make Love to You?	200
I Can't Get Enough of You	202
Phenomenal King	204
Putting Your Expectations to Rest	206
Who am I?	209
My Royal Party	211
My Wonderland	213
Our Conversation	215
Tic-Toc Tic-Toc	218
Erase Your Pain	220
One Special Day	221
The Greatest Gift	223
I Won't Settle	225
My Love Divine	226
Secret Stories Untold	227
I Will Make You Fall in Love	229
Until You Climax	231
You Have Awakened My Love...	233
I Can't Sleep Without You	236
For Eternity	238
If I...	240
My Heart and Soul	244
One of a Kind	246
The Love of My Life	250
Her Empty Space	252
About the Author	257

I Can't Resist

In the still of the evening without sunlight to intrude, I see the twilight in your eyes, as the moon sets up the mood, playing music softly and low, this will be an everlasting show, as romance fills the air, I can't help but feel aroused the very moment you came near, you submit to my warm embrace while candles flicker their flames, after tonight you won't be the same, the smell of your perfume drives my love insane, it's a feeling I can't explain, a feeling **I Can't Resist**, allowing your love to rain down on me, this opportunity I could not miss, staring into your eyes while running my fingers through your hair, I smell the sweetness of your neck as I nibble at your ear, I'm overjoyed with love, with you I have no fear, whispering words of love that fills your ear as you answer with a sigh, this will be an unforgettable ride, your sexy body starts to come alive, you're the heat of my desire, the spark to my fire as we slowly come undressed laying you down as you welcome my caress, rubbing on your sexy curves, your body, your love is what I deserve, a taste **I Can't Resist**, your breasts show a response when I touch with a kiss, as I soak inside your love giving you that ultimate rush, you feeling my thrashing in all my back-and-forth action, your eyes are closed here comes that satisfaction, my love **I Can't Resist** your love passion.

Be with You

*All I want to do is be with you, come into your life and show you that love is real, this is what I feel, playing infield not out, let King show you what he's about, without a doubt I can make you scream and shout, but that's too easy baby be easy baby, believe me you will score, this heart of mine is yours, let me show you love deep down from my core, then our love making will mean so much more, kissing you with passion as I go in and out, thrusting, everlasting, giving that body a good thrashing,(pause) as I grab my glass of Ciroc to take another sip before I continue to move and dip into your love, thighs and hips, yes you feel you see that I'm fully equipped your juices flowing filling up, I have your body on tilt, as we keep going and going, you enjoying every position being submissive loving my kisses, my sheets soak and wet from the rain showers you dishing, tonight we on a different type of a mission, I won't stop until your finished, satisfaction will be given, my love is never ending, each time will feel like the beginning, the first time you became mine, even frozen in time my heart will beat for you no matter what I will always **Be With You**, my love is forever true when it comes to you..*

Loved in my Kitchen

Awakened by the smell of food, I found my Queen cooking in the nude, I step behind her kissing her neck, she smiles turns around and say wait baby not just yet the food is almost done your plate will be set, whispers of no baby I can't wait I crave your sex, turning you around lifting you high setting you on the counter for a royal surprise, kissing you slow our bodies are close holding you tight and never letting go, hands on your thighs touching your prize, a diamond in the rough as my index finger gives your palace a thrust, I love you so much, a rush of passion going through your veins a feeling you can't explain, my tongue going down to that perfect place driving you insane, you begin to scratch and moan calling my name, telling me I ease your pain, as your palace begins to shiver and shake you scream keep licking me that way, baby forever stay as I play with your clit, I stand and rub your palace with the tip of my royal stick, teasing you before I enter your pleasure hole, giving you everything, going deep reaching your soul, showing you I can play all types of roles, picking you up and putting you on the kitchen floor, spreading you wide as I slide in giving you that yellow light (slow), so you feel all my might, you're enjoying my show, I'm doing everything just right, going deeper and deeper taking you off the floor bending you over the kitchen sink, giving you more and more, my goddess it's you whom I adore, your screams are louder than you think, you got the neighbors knocking at the door, as you bust all over me, not paying them no attention, your body I continue to explore, kissing you from your shoulders to your back as I give you that royal attack loving that arch you put in your back pulling your hair as I go deep within, screams and shouts of I'm about to cum again, words of I'm almost there baby beware I'm going to explode, keep hitting it right there, you can't hold it as you let it go, you're loving my rhythm loving my royal show, my legs begin to shake, wobble and roll, exploding my love deep down into your soul, saying I love you and I will never let you go, for with you I am whole, I feel you deep down in my soul, whispers of I will never let you go, never will we separate from each other's love, our soul is one, cherishing this love for all time, baby you are the epitome of fine, for the rest of my lifetime I will give it to you right, making love every day and night putting it down acting a fool when I'm inside of you, I know what you need I got the power to feed you for eternity, can't you see? Making love to you is what I was put on this earth to do, my love will never die, subside, for you, I cannot hide this lifetime ride.

King's Love

The time has come, for you to bring your body here, near, close to mine let's not waste any more time, in my mind you have been mine in so many different ways, I will show you my love has no limits, it will make you misbehave, once I'm deep into your cave, my love will take you outer space, grabbing you by the waist as I kiss the side of your face, sliding over to your lips, loving the way you sway your hips, ready, set, go, kissing you nice and slow, (blinds open) who cares let's give the neighbors a show, right now your mind, body, and soul is all I know, whispers of give me what I've been waiting for my heart is yours, feed me more, open up, let me into your pleasure store so that I can touchdown and score, as I pull you down to the floor slowly licking you low until you feel that undying flow, welcome to **King's Love** show, scratching while you moan in that sexy tone, you are where you belong, this love can't be wrong, making love to you with my tongue, you screaming out I'm about to cum, King's got your body hotter than the sun, as I lick inside and out, you're busting like a gun, screams and shouts comes from your mouth, our hearts equals one, you come second to none you are my one, as I stand to slide in between those thick thighs, to no surprise you have my kingdom on rise, I look deep into your eyes when I start to push inside, without a doubt I am everlasting, no cameras, no acting, this is real love satisfaction, loving every move every action, going all night until the morning sun, I still have your body busting like a gun, showing you that **King's Love** is number one, nobody can compare, even come close to the way I do your body, I swear **King's Love** is a drug, turning you into a fiend, making you come back for more losing track of time, days and months, **King's Love** is the only thing you will want to explore, the only thing on your mind, you adore the way I unwind your body, love and passion the thoughts rolling through you can't fight it, you're loving the way I push inside it, inside of you, making you fall deep in love with the things I do, I am your gift sent from above straight to you, this is true love, I'm not even wearing a glove, this love, my love you can't get enough of, your love out shines the sun, no I am not done, I can keep going for months and months at a time, **King's Love** is not a lie, time is on our side, never will we run out, there's no doubt your love is what I'm all about, your love is all mine for the rest of our lives I will be at your side, this is a natural high that's taking you past the skies on top of the clouds, now you understand why I wear this crown, in your eyes I can see your heart smile, I can see your soul dancing around happy you have found this drug called **King's Love**.

My Dream Girl

Arose from a vision in my mind that was so vivid, so divine, this girl was the essence of sex appeal, so fine, the smell of her perfume had me on a natural high, this girl was so bad, with her sexy thighs, had me amazed, I'm going insane it's her whole body I crave, to feel, see, smell, taste, touch I begin to blush loving the rush she gives me when the day retires at its latest hour, closing my eyes to no surprise my beautiful Queen is right by my side each and every night I can't wait to close my eyes, to be awakened by your lips, touching my soul with a kiss, filled with passion can you image how this gift may feel, this love is real, my dream has become my reality, never will I wake, the vision of you I can't shake, my heart will break without your love, we go hand and hand like a glove, you are my dove and I am your eagle soaring high in the sky each and every night, wondering what you will have in store for me when I turn out my lights, your my wife, my Queen, **My Dream Girl**, I love our world that we share in reality or fantasy you are where I want to be, your love I will forever seek, through my eyes you can see, that you are the only one for me, with you I am complete.

You're a Love Freak

I'm a **Love Freak** like a Scorpio, but nevertheless I am Mr. Romantic Virgo, the affection of this Virgo is like no other, the way I show love will make you pause and wonder, unpredictable is what you will be saying, no complaining when I touch you, a trail of roses and candles to the bedroom just for you, I want nothing more than to be with you, you blowing me away the way those hips sway, holding your body close, from coast to coast I rip, brag and boast about your love, I'm your fiend and your my drug sent from heaven above my beautiful dove, as I bring your love wall down, royalty on high when King Mr. Romantic Virgo in between those thighs, left and right, as I'm thrusting with my tongue this won't be a short night, around and around this feeling is oh so right, flicks of the candlelight music on slow, speechless you are as I go low, while on my knees pulling you close doing the most as I lick your pleasure boat, giving you that all night show, a marathon to the stars and beyond off that Remy V, do you think you can handle my **Love Freak**? Once in between these sheets I become a different person, a different freak, love takes over me, I will have you weak as I creep in between your knees, I want nothing more than to be **Your Love Freak**, pleasing your every desire, we will be going for hours, my **Love Freak** doesn't have a time limit, this is just the beginning, giving you something you've never seen before, the way I explode every inch of your body I will have you so excited, you won't be able to fight it, those words you thought you would never say will come out from hiding, King I love you and everything you do, you say, as I thrust away there's no escape no place you would rather be in this world than with me in between these sheets, I'm giving you everything you have been looking for, not taking this experience for granted, passionate kisses are exchanged it's hard for your feelings to manage, you becoming my wife is on your mind, knowing that you will never come to find another **Love Freak** of my kind, giving you everything you desire when I'm in between those thighs, don't be surprise, I can and I will make you explode all night, climaxing high to the skies, as a single tear falls from your left eye, then another falls from your right, you're whispering in my ear, baby this love is all mine, keep pushing inside, I'm glad I came to find you my **Love Freak**, your heart, body and soul belongs to me, you got me weak, I love everything you're doing to me, as you soak up my sheets, I do nothing but please and please nobody can out do me, **Your Love Freak**, once you enter inside my sheets.

Everlasting

Thinking of the time we will spend, ***Everlasting****, never will our love end, Everlasting, a knock at the door, it is you, I wait a second, (take a sip of my drink) to calm down my groove, (opening the door with smiles) please come in, a kiss on the cheek as you pass, taking your bags telling you to go to the bathroom and relax, (thinking to myself, I been playing this night over and over in my mind my beautiful find, I snapping back into time), your queendom awaits, steaming hot bath, rose pedals and candles just for you to cure any aches, at last Stella Rosa poured in a glass, closing the door saying I will be waiting for your sexy ass,* ***Everlasting****, minutes pass feel like hours, I can't wait to devour, conquer your body, I'm so excited, but need to play it cool, I can't wait any longer, I feel so much for you (knocking on the door) ready to show you what I can do, ready to explore, (door swings open) you walk out in your teddy and heels, I see you're not playing it's time to get real, come have a drink with me as we continue to relax and chill, sitting close making a toast to an* ***Everlasting*** *night as I gaze into your eyes moving my hands up towards your thighs, body nice and smooth, I'm in this groove called you, my feelings shooting through the ceiling, straight to the moon, back to the room where you find me on top of you, kissing and rubbing giving you all my loving,* ***Everlasting****, our hearts beating and rushing, long soft gentle stroking, our bodies in motion, passion is burning, you yearning for more, I give you a* deep thrust as I yell and roar, you're on climax number three as I go low to give you a treat, blessing you with my tongue, words falling from your mouth I'm the one, **Everlasting**, when I'm down south, like the sun going down and a volcano erupts, I'm giving you more of this number one, but we're not done, turn around for more fun, more climaxing giving that ass a good thrashing, once again I'm **Everlasting**, this was your ultimate test, as I lay your body for its final rest, until next time we meet to repeat this **Everlasting** affair, leaving a lasting impression so you keep thinking of the love we share, **Everlasting**, can't nobody tell me anything or compare, you got me flying high, soaring disappearing into thin air, I never want to come down from here, this love will be, is **Everlasting**, when I'm with you it's heaven sent, baby you are the realist, can't nobody replace you and the things you do, you got my body going numb the way you kiss me I feel so much love, I am now and forever will be your **Everlasting**, number one.

My World

*If you were in **My World** tonight there's no way you could resist or fight when I my do once I begin to touch you and put you in my love groove, here's a taste of the passion I feel for you and what I will do to that beautiful body of yours, here's a preview, after tonight you will tell me my heart is yours, for I don't ever what to be without you my love it's you I adore, as we get ready to get down, I'm going to take you to a new level, a King like me you never been around, I'm going to take you to the next level in your life, your body is my town, you ready to become my wife, my Queen?, And hold down everything that world means, we're throwing out all jacks and jokers, just us King and Queen making your royal dream become your reality, I'm going to give you all of me, take my hand and just follow me, I will lead you to the land of ecstasy, give me your heart and I'll will love you for eternity, from my body to my soul with you **My World** is whole, **My World** is complete, holding you close and never letting go, without you I am weak, your heart is mines, my heart is yours this I know I'm putting on a show, pulling you in with my eyes rubbing on those curves moving towards those thighs, as we groove in this rhythm called your love, pleasing you is a must, I'm taking my time with you my beautiful flower, my beautiful dove, there's no reason to rush, I can go for hours, kissing you softly, picking you up gently and carrying you to the shower, making you wetter as I devour your body, you're* a cold piece of work, the way you're throwing it back as I push inside it, you got me on the defense while you attack, you working that back showing King where it's at, water going everywhere as I pull your hair roughly, letting go inside of you is ever so tempting, caressing your neck with my tongue as I go deeper where no light shows not even the sun can go where I'm going, I got your juices flowing and flowing, a waterfall is what you're showing, in **My World** I can keep going and going, pleasing you until the day retires its skies and the stars begin to shine big and bright, from the shower to the room that's filled with roses and candlelight, soft music plays as you become my sexual slave, it feels like we have been going for days, I have you amazed, you all twisted up in a daze, pleasing you all night, I'm loving the way you rock the mic, this love is outta sight, you feel my power, you feel my might, if only I had you in **My World** tonight, I know you won't hesitate to become my wife, my loving is just that right, you don't need to put up any kind of fight, this love will live on and on for the rest of your life.

Unbelievable

The things I can do to your body are **Unbelievable**, you will think it's a dream the way I'm making you fiend, you will think my love is make believe, but this is no dream, this is reality not a fantasy, so hop aboard of this fantastic voyage of ecstasy and enjoy the ride for this may be the last time King blesses you tonight, I will be leaving you a lasting impression as we begin with this session, your my student, I'm about to teach you a lesson, this loving making is my profession, in your mind you can tell I was sent from heaven, the way my touch is ever so soft, you're wishing and hoping this is not the last time I rip your panties off, touching your canvas with my lips and tongue, kissing and licking has you burning hot like fire, I stop, drop and roll you are my desire, deep down into your soul I go taking control of your body, mind and heart as I float deep inside, taking you on this journey, the ride of your life I will make you bust more than twice, tonight is your night, as I continue to push inside, you loving everything I do, your passion begins to rise and rise, satisfaction is guaranteed when I'm giving you my groove, moans going through my ears as I make love to you, anticipating my next move you are, knowing I can take you to the moon past the stars, beautiful is what you are, check what I can do as I take you high and above, to a place where you will never be able to get enough of my love as I go low giving you an **Unbelievable** show with my tongue, (hold up we're not done check my remix) as I stand, grab and flip you upside down showing you why I wear this crown, I got your love shooting up, but coming down as I lick around and around in and out making you scream and shout, you're stroking me with your mouth showing me what your about, I got you adapting to this **Unbelievable** freaky situation, laying you down on the bed gently so that you can feel this sexual sensation as I French kiss you sweetly before penetration, now I'm pushing into you deeply, you complete me falls off your tongue, the time, it's past one, it's closer to the sun coming up as your body erupts, with every touch with every thrust I have your legs shaking, the backboard of the bed is breaking, you exploding uncontrollably as I continue to slow stroke your soaking wet palace, you never thought or could imagine the feelings you feel right now could be real, you love it when I'm playing in your field, coming back for more you will this I know, you love it when I come around to give you that **Unbelievable** show.

Deep Dreaming

*My love Runs Deep, tell me can you see yourself with a guy like me? A King sitting high above the clouds in the sky, close your eyes and you will find me moving slow kissing you from head to toe, holding you tight as I push inside with all my might, going all night giving you what you like, this loving is just right, for you, for me, can't you see, opening your eyes don't be surprised if you still feel me inside, I told you My Love Runs Deep even when you sleep you **Dream** of me, inside of your palace can you image, me going Deep until I reach your soul, making you fiend and feel whole, treating your body more precious than gold, putting your legs up like touchdown, what is this you found? A King that's better than the rest of those clowns that you have been around, round and round we go telling me don't stop keep hitting me in that spot, changing positions so you can climb on top, I got your palace hotter than a sweat shop, burning calories, kissing your neck as you screaming out this is the best sex I've ever had, waking up glad, pinching yourself wishing it wasn't a **Dream**, but yet reality sets in, thinking about the next time we will meet again..*

Thoughts of You

Sitting in this midnight hour, **Thoughts of You** my beautiful flower crosses my mind, loving you more and more each and every time I hold you close, kissing you slow letting go that's a no, my heart is yours this I can say, never will I leave no storm will get in our way, I will work through those raining days just to stay with you, my love is true, it flows deep from the top of my head to the bottom of my feet, I can't wait for the day we meet at the altar, under are Heavenly Father we will go further and beyond, our love will continue to live on and on even long after we are gone, with time this love will grow stronger and stronger, this I know, this is a lifetime show, with any other woman I would have been done and moved on to the next one, but **Thoughts of You** I can't shake, you have the mind of a teacher and I'm loving your Coca Cola shape, this bond we cannot break, testifying to the preacher, that this vow I take, I will stand by her side for the rest of my days, after looking into her eyes I've been hooked from within, without her I can't win, with you I'm all in giving up the game breaking down and choosing you to have and forever wear my crown and run my town I'm giving you my last name, so cherish and hold it down, my soul mate in you is what I have found, my number one love, our destiny has just begun, everything I will do will be for you, for love,, my blessing, my angel you have me wrapped up, this I know I could never get enough of the **Thoughts** of my beautiful flower, who holds the power to love and conquer my heart and soul, to the depths of hell I will go for your love for you I will do anything to show you I just want to please you, believe me when I tell you I need you in my life, I don't need or want anybody else to become my wife, there's no substitute for your love you are heaven sent, a special dove from above made just for me, you are all I need close and next to me, just one little **Thought of You** sends my mind in a frenzy, you have a spell on me that I don't want to break, I ache when you're away, you complete my days, tell me you will forever stay, I couldn't live if you ever took your love away, these **Thoughts of You** turn into actions when you are near I have no fear with you being by my side, my feelings I can't hide I can't say it enough I need you in my life, you have me on a natural high flying fast, this love will outlast my past, I thank my past, for at last my heart is not hiding behind its mask anymore with one knee to the floor, showing you I want to forever be yours..

Royal Room

Passion is the sign you will see flashing above the door of my **Royal Room**, there's so much I will do once you step inside, first take my hand as I sweep you off your feet like a broom, looking into your sexy brown eyes softly, I can feel your heart beating calmly, kissing your lips gently as I take you on this Royal trip, a trip you will never forget, causing your passion to rise as my hands slide up and down your body, caressing you slowly, I'm reading your road signs I see where you want me to go, your arrows are pointing down below, as I stick shift through your curves with my tongue, you're in a room that's hotter than the sun, I'm seeing signs of walk please don't run it's slippery when wet and I'm not trying to crash just yet, I begin breaking a sweat as I come up for air, your passion just flowing going everywhere, causing a flood and we just begun and that was only the use of my tongue, it's time to put in more work pulling off my shirt, you watching me flex, a sign on my chest with arrows pointed down saying, you haven't seen nothing yet, as I pull out damage I hope you can manage, kissing you roughly and turning your back towards the front of me, I arch your back and put that thang in reverse, as you grab the pillow and clutch the sheets, no this is not rehearsed, no script, you watching me in the mirror as I rip back and forth inside of you, screams of I'm loving every stroke each time you coast I feel you low, grabbing at your hips as I flow and flow, spreading you apart so I can go deeper go far into your palace did you ever image my **Royal Room** will have you in this type of groove, have you in this type of mood, with this type of King, who's making all your dreams coming true, giving you everything, showing you your worth in every move I do, you are a goddess walking this earth, flipping you to the side as we continue this Royal ride, you enjoying the motions as I push inside your love, one leg up my sexy dove as I set up with a soft but hard thrust going deeper is a must, rolling you to your back so you could feel me deep as I attack, two legs up on my shoulders going longer and longer, looking into your eyes as I'm giving you that Royal treatment, your knees weaken and bending as I slip and slide inside, you're winning from beginning to ending, I'm never finished until you finish taking you higher than the stars, in my **Royal Room** I can, I will take you far, precious, my love you are, by far the best thing to step in my **Royal Room**, I see you can handle everything I do, is this true, could it really be you, my Queen I mean, I've been searching for my perfect fit, my perfect find, never will I tap or quit, you will always be mine, I must admit your love is the shit, you are the one I was put on this earth to be with.

Body to Body

*I want us to be **Body to Body**, don't try and fight it, you nor I can hide it, you should know my thoughts, **Body to Body** my sexy hottie can't wait to stretch you out like Pilates and go about it licking all over your, **Body to Body** got me feeling naughty as I open the door to your party, I'm so glad I was invited, now face to Body traveling your avenues, got you feeling X-rated so faded off this drug called King, tongue to Body giving you that royal thing that royal pleasure I can last forever as long as we are **Body to Body** our hearts are one, our souls shines brighter than the sun, we're heaven's glow when we're **Body to Body**, none can compare to you or your show, a gift from above I'm so in love, going into your Body soft and gentle putting it down your face holds no frowns, but a smile while pushing **Body to Body**, my love we fit tight like some gloves to the moon and above, while we're **Body to Body** on a cloud called love, your moans are singing pretty like a blue mocking bird, I'm loving every word that rolls of your tongue, you're the one when we're **Body to Body** I don't want nobody, but you, I don't need my crew, I'm flying with you, I'm loving when your back to my Body can't nobody interrupt this party, I'm drunk but not off Bacardi, it's your **Body to Body** that has me excited, that has me intoxicated, I'm loving the way you ride it when you're on top of my Body, I don't have a care in the world, because I have you my girl, holding you close as you smile with every* stroke got me ready to explode into you while we're **Body to Body** giving you all my power as you devour my Body French kissing while listening to you moan, we're not worrying about any phones when we're **Body to Body** I am where I belong, in between your thighs is my throne, while **Body to Body** I call your heart my home, reaching new heights encouraging my confidence while **Body to Body**, treating you like royalty, I will swim any sea if it meant you will be there waiting for my Body to be next to your Body, making my day every time you say you love me, blowing my mind high past the skies, you are so fine, unwinding your Body each and every time, I will always find time to please you, your vibe has me in a groove that I don't want to lose, I love this mood and everything about you, your love has me flying past the stars to the moon and back, you have my love showing different attacks when we come close enough to be **Body to Body**, I can't hide nor can't fight it, your love I just have to be inside it when we become **Body to Body**.

Enter Your Love

As soon as I **Enter Your Love** we hear them knock, knock, knocking on the walls, but don't be alarmed, they will bring you no harm, as I proceed to breaking headboards going hard when in between those halls, neighbors continue screaming threatening to call the law, as I slide through the walls of love, passion so deep kissing you taste so sweet as I pull out to go low in between these sheets, in between those knees, one touch and I already hear cries and moans of I'm getting weak, your thighs tighten squeezing my cheeks as I play with your pearl tongue, what's this I see, your legs start shaking your body has been waiting, for me to come and bring you stimulation, licking you in that right places hitting all your spots, more cries from the neighbors about calling the cops, giving you some instructions, baby put that pillow on top of your mouth we got haters around our house, I love when you scream and shout while I'm pleasing you down south, going deep into your space, invading I am taking my place, in control of your heart, body and soul you feel complete and whole, when I'm holding you close, I will cherish you from the bottom of my soul, never letting you go, **Entering Your Love** with some powerful stuff, I will forever have a hold on you, to my love groove you will surrender, yes there will always be contenders stepping up to your plate, but just remember they are just pretenders, they are not me and can't have you weak the way I have you weak in between these sheets, you only need my love freak and the way that I creep, I got you buzzing drunk off my love flying higher and above while inside of your love I can't do no wrong, listening to that song, twelve play following everything Mr. Kelly says, but still doing things my way, making you say this is the best I have ever had up to this date, as I'm bringing your love wall down, as we go round and round, I'm glad it's you I've found, you loving the way I'm making you rain taking away all your pain, driving your mind, body, heart and soul insane with the way I'm pushing inside of you, we're face to face so you can't hide when I'm gazing into your eyes as I fill you up inside, this is a long drive, I have enough fuel to ride for two days and two nights, our loving, our everything is just right when I **Enter Your Love** my heaven sent from up above, I adore you so much, you're all that I think of I need your touch, I need your body, mind, heart and soul to make me complete, to make me whole, I will forever sing this song, my heart belongs with you this is a for sure thing you are my Queen and I am your King I will love you through any and everything.

Dream Catcher

I dream of you each night, thoughts of you being in my life consume me, you come to see me on any given night, entering my world when I close my eyes to no surprise it's you I see, sexy from your head to your pretty little feet, your smile has me going wild, going crazy, tossing and turning yearning for your love, as I extend for your hand trust I have that royal plan letting you know once you walk through these doors you will be in lovers land, as we walk through the doors you see nothing, but rose pedals on the floor, on the bed, is where you are led, lighting candles I am as you slowly undress, I'm saying leave those heels on and let me take off your thong it's about to be on, a showdown as I lay your body down back exposed starting with a kiss towards your neck, rubbing your body down giving you pleasure without hitting you with my lasting endeavor just yet, (we haven't got to that part, you can bet this is and will be your number one sex), sending chills up and down your spine, my **Dream Catcher** you are so fine, your beauty blows my mind each and every time I close my eyes, making my way towards your thighs never having a night of surprise like this, but check my mix as I start to kiss and lick, and candles flick and flick, I have your body in a twist, going deep getting it in, your legs start to shake and bend this is some different love making with me you will win, screaming and scratching, moaning while we groaning taking away my stress every time I lay to rest my sweet beautiful **Dream Catcher**, I am a mess when not with you, I take daily naps just to catch you, I can never be the same again my love only knows you, I love everything about you, my dreams feel so true as I'm banging on your body going deeper inside you, I'm taking you there you're calling out my name you not giving no complaints, I'm making you rain, just you and me is all I can see, your love will never be the same, it's time for a position change, I want to sleep for days, I can live in a coma forever, if it meant you will forever be my love slave, for the rest of my life becoming my wife, my Queen you shine so bright, you mean everything, the world to me wishing I can bring you out of my darkness into the light, but I know that cannot happen so I'll be sure to catch, you my **Dream Catcher** each and every night.

Another Man's Girl

We met some time ago, I never forgot that show, late night I think of you and only you being the King of my throne, that's the text that came through to my phone, I reply you know where you belong when are you going to come home, high is what I will have you, mind gone in the clouds, my style is very different each time we meet I show out, show you how love's supposed to feel when pleasuring your spouse, listening to you moan sounds like a sweet love song (as your house phone rings), you says hello! By no surprise it's the other guy crying out it can't be over I love you without a doubt, can I come see you, let me come to the house, She pause then says, no not right now I have company I'm going to be busy for a while, I'll get back with you, before hanging up (a loud FUCK, from the other end of the phone), he cries out! It's King isn't it? silence, this can't be true now I know you're gone forever, that King character is real clever hanging up saying I'm going to show him I'm better, drinking his pain away in anger, in rage, meanwhile I'm pleasing you in many different ways with that smile upon your face, grabbing at my waist you are as I pull in straight this is just the beginning of a long day, hope you have some time for what I'm about to put your body through, it's time for me to show and prove, as I put it down, this may take a while, blessed you are to be in my town, giving you a piece of my crown, showing you a different type of love, a love from outer space and above, them *feelings you feeling inside you can't hide it, your emotions won't let you fight it, tell me how you want it, and I will provide it, I'm at your mercy, I'm following your every command, you are in King's hands as I stroke and touch with your legs wrap around my waist, a squeeze by your thighs as you grab and tug pulling me deeper into your place, with your hands on my butt, your expressions shows that you can't get enough, my love has taken over your emotions inside as you explode with passion I can see the satisfaction in your eyes, we laugh and cuddle lying in bed as time passes us by, these words I cry, I will never cease to give you love and take away your pain, you're in my heart these are not games, with me you will never be the same, making love to you for here on out, leaving you with nothing to complain about, nothing but passionate screams and shouts, moaning from the night to the early morning, you say then bring it on I will forever sing your song, heavy knocking comes upon your door, sounds like a man looking to settle a score you look startled and I'm like awe shit it must be that man that you was fooling with, I say awe shit, as I slide my pants on lock and load in with the clip just in case he wants to trip, she say you don't know who it could be hold up don't flip, opening up the door, we both look at each other and I say I can't believe this shit. (To be continued).*

My Experience with a Queen

Never have I ever experienced anything so overwhelming, so intense, so sexually demanding, your body is so pleasing to my eyes, the epitome of a woman's sexuality you have taken my love by surprise, when my eyes take in all that splendid nakedness, I tend to feel a familiar stiffness in my boxer briefs as we climb into the sheets you kissing and rubbing all over me, taking control you are, never have I had to play the part, play the role of being submission, I'm loving your luscious kisses, your tongue taste delicious, you taking me there, to another level, only way I can explain is that you have me hotter that the devil, as I'm pulling on your hair from my back as you ride and attack your head goes back as you arch your back, giving me that ultimate test showing me your best, rest assured you making me want more and more, I don't need no rest as I start to kiss and suck on your breasts, our sheets has become a mess, your body is stealing the show as you hop off top and go low giving me a Queen show, you got me on a float, you rocking my boat as your lips wrap around my royal pole, I touch your throat, damn you're bad no gag, no choke deeper I go, your mouth slides up and down my pole showing me you're in control taking your time, taking it slow, how far will you go, I'm gazing at all of you loving everything you're doing, forever your love I will be pursuing, your complexion puts me in heaven, beautiful light creaminess compels me to taste, as you come up and kiss me on the cheek of my face, our lips graze sending off a blaze, a fire all through my body and my soul, this **Experience with a Queen** I will never let go, you have my body in a haze, my mind in a daze from the love we have made, from the love we shared, I can't find this love anywhere, can't no woman compare to **My Experience with my Queen**, you are my everything and so much more, I'm loving the way you explore my body, nobody could ever handle it or ride it, I'm so excited for what's to come, you are my one and only, I've been waiting for you for so long, for your body, to call you my own, I fit perfect when inside it, tell me you will never leave me alone, to you I belong, for the rest of my life I will fight and fight with all my strength, with all my might for your love with all the power sent from above, each and every night, this love is so divine, so right, I will love **My Experience with a Queen** for life.

My Magic Love Show

From the moment I walk into the club, I see this shine, a bright light, a glow of a woman that I want, that I have to have tonight, catching eyes was the sign I needed, now I know I won't be defeated, as I glide over staring at your curves, in my mind I'm going berserk, going crazy, I want to be inside your skirt, DJ keep playing that song, I'm loving the way she's working those hips, baby girl has an aura so strong as I get close enough to catch your next dip, grooving and moving with your every twist, turning you around to get a full glimpse of this beautiful miss, DJ please slow it down, it's time for me to flip the script, it's time for me to take you on a Magic trip, as we dance slowly I'm pulling you close, holding you tight this feeling is nice, my hands dropping low, tonight is are night, I got your body hot I'm the one, looking into your eyes they're shining brighter than sun, my eyes relaxing you, hypnotize is what I do, blushing you are as you start to feel light, not knowing we took flight dancing above the crowd, I have you feeling free and wild, as we burst into a cloud of smoke, I welcome you to my palace, sit back and watch me Do Magic, you're closing your eyes letting go as I give you a glass to make a toast to **My Magic Love Show**, I am your King sent from heaven above, inside my world it's my show, you don't have to worry your admission is already paid for, it's you I adore, from the floor to the couch, kissing you more and more, no reason to doubt, nice and slow from your neck towards your perfectly shaped breasts I go, giving your soft but hard nipples a show, making your body move and ripple, touching you low your body has this incredible glow, pressing you up against the door, your body is my map, yes I'm exploring, sex with this King is never boring, going all night until the morning and even then I'm still not done exploring, as I remix my love, sweet passion sweating down your frame I'm taking aim, all smiles, no complaints, glad you are I came into your world invading your space, digging the way I handle your body as I take my place, you're feeling my groove, lighting your soul on fire, fulfilling your every desire I am, going deeper and deeper inside it, your love is in the mood, you're loving the way I'm rocking it, you can't fight it, your heart has decided, you're busting so much as I push inside it, this love is undying, it's written all over your face, no man have ever made you feel this way, real love making I can say, you will never be loved in this way by another, you're bent over the bed clinching the covers, as I dig through your tunnel of love, you're making me twist and dip as I feel my gun getting ready to unload his clip, I'm letting it go as I explode into a cloud of smoke back into the club we go, dancing slow to that same song loving every bit of **My Magic Show** while dancing in my arms..

In Due Time, You will be Mine

Getting closer and closer to making you mine, I've been waiting for so long to call you my own, I'm so ready to come home to a woman of your stature, my Queen you are everything to me, can't you tell, you are where I want to be, holding you close at night in between the sheets, you climbing all over my throne, showing me your love in many ways and different forms, don't be alarmed you're in King's arms, never will I hurt you my Queen, I was hoping you came along, like an answer to my prayer, lyrics to a song this is where you belong with me can't you see, this night will change our lives forever like a fantasy of mine, I told you **In Due Time, You Will Be Mine**, at the time I never knew your name and now that I have found you my heart will never be the same, so pardon if I stare at the fantasy I once knew before, it's you who I adore, you're on climax number four giving you more and more, thanking God for this angel He has sent to me, looking into your eyes with joy shining brighter than the sunlight, the day will come when I make you my wife, for life, is that alright? **In Due Time, You Will Be Mine** never will you find a man like me rocking your boat like we're sailing the seven seas as we lay to rest falling asleep in my arms it's like heaven's peace, my heart beats within your chest.

My Throne

Your love is my scripture, I'm following every encryption to crack your code, to forever know the truth of your heart and the love that you hold deep down inside, I can see right through your beautiful eyes my hold you can trust, I hold no lies, this is not lust but love, laying you down on **My Throne**, kissing you slowly making you feel welcome, **My Throne** is your Throne to have and to own, my Queen on high as I take your body for a ride tonight is our night, no more running from it, no more denying it, I won't tap or quit, you the realist I've ever been with, sealing this moment with a kiss to your frontal lobe, you sigh and exhale ready to let go, continue to kiss I do, letting you know any wish you make will come true, my heart belongs to you, I'm nominating you, I will do whatever you want me to do, just you and me not worrying about a thing as I continue to put these flawless moves on your frame making your love rain down, showering all over me, you're saying **My Throne** is where you're supposed to be, as we creep, creep, creep underneath the sheets, screams of you feel so good inside of me, don't stop give it all to me your Queen wants to ride your love machine, (switching positions), taking it to a different level, I see you on a new mission putting your gears in motion, grabbing at my stick shift to get you rolling, now you're in control I'm going deep as you drop low I'm touching your soul, setting a blaze through your body, you're beaming up to Scotty, but on a natural high I can't lie you're curling my toes riding me right just like I like your love is outta sight, you're arching your back bouncing slow, your hair hanging low, (changing positions) here we go as I begin to steal the show, I start by going back where I've already been be before, my tongue low licking slow, (listening to Trey Songs "You Belong"), making you bust right in the middle of the song, playing with your pearl tongue giving you that number one, body busting and erupting as I French kiss your hot wet oven, giving you all my loving, I begin to crawl up your sexy thighs to no surprise my royal is still at a rise filling your insides, kissing slowly while pushing low, soft and gentle, rocking your boat, giving you **My Throne** treatment, while holding you close and tight making sure you feel all my might and power in every thrust, my type of loving will have you go back to your girls with a blush as you discuss, my love will become a must, as I slide back and forth into your palace giving you that everlasting love, all that you could imagine, everything that you could ever dream of, going all night long, your heart equals my love, as we lay to sleep the night away in **My Throne**.

Office Love

The day is getting late, you have been working so hard you didn't even realize it was already past eight, calling home telling your husband you will be home a little late, without knowing your crush walks by, your fantasies begin to take place, you bat your eyes in a sexy way, but in that professional tone leaves from your lips, hi crossing your thighs underneath your desk as you stare at my chest, setting your soul on fire, nevertheless, I reply with a hi and a smile saying I'm working on that new case file I'm going to be here for a while, I was just grabbing some coffee, as I'm talking and talking you're not hearing anything I say, going off into this place of love, looking at my lips, licking yours while blowing a kiss, you're thinking I wish you would come and toss me, show me who's in charge, boss me, standing up and coming from behind your desk asking do I need any help, with a sway in your hips a lick of your lips, a sip of my coffee I take, as you move closer this way I say, but before I can form any words a finger of yours goes over my lips your eyes are telling me we're about to take a trip, you're starting to upload my computer chip, sparks are flying like the fourth of July fireworks to the sky, this sexual attraction is undying, my heart you are satisfying, slowly unbuttoning my shirt and unbuckling my pants, raising one leg of yours, you fulfilling one dream, tonight you will score, your thigh against my thigh, you grabbing my hand sliding it up your skirt showing me your worth hottest river running here on earth, I turned your desk into my personnel space, clearing it off laying you down face to face, I slide in filling your space, I'm seeing the satisfaction upon your face, tonight this love you won't be able to erase, you will store it safely in a hidden place, taking more control grabbing you at the waist lifting you off the desk now we're chest to chest, your legs cradle in my arms as I start to perform, hitting you with this thunder and lightning storm, making you bust rapidly, this is nothing like the norm, putting you down on your own two feet, turning you around so I can see that nice soft round kissing you before I start to put it down, you thinking to yourself look at what I have found, pulling at your hair turning your face around, so that I can see that smile, standing you straight up so you can feel me deep, kissing at your neck your legs begin to feel weak, you at your peek, but you snap back into reality where you're still sitting behind your desk listening to me speak, me not knowing you were sitting there fantasizing about me, your **Office Love**.

Formal Invite

Meeting you on this local website exchanging numbers texting and talking each and every night, the time has come for me to give you a **Formal Invite**, you accept hurrying over as I set the mood just right, doorbell rings it's you, I'm walking to the door at ease and calm with nothing but my jeans and Timberlands on, opening up the door I started at the floor, my eyes to your pretty feet on to your sexy legs and thighs in my mind I'm already adoring thee, saying my, my, my, I have been blessed on this cold winter night, looking at those hips that don't quit, as well as a nice ass to go along with, I must admit we are about to go on a love making tip, after I'm done you will admit that your feelings have flipped, in my direction, saying you have graduated and professing your love for me to the rest and you're loving this situation is what you will attest to, as my eyes go past those sexy curves, I'm digging everything about you, a pure heart is what you deserve, I will be pouring out nothing but love, I have found what I've been dreaming of, gazing at those voluptuous breasts, I can't wait to suck on, to lick on, to show you the way that I perform while holding you close to my chest, this will be nothing like the norm, finally rising to see your beautiful brown eyes, now I can see your gorgeous face, I start to feel a rise in my pants, there's no more time to waste, you can take the crown now, give me your hand and come with me, you have an aura that glows abundantly, never have I seen someone so beautiful, pleasantly I say, please come inside, it's already past nine, but who's worried about the time, I pull you close, closer to me, to my lips locking eyes before we kiss, eruption, explosive my touch is making you do the most I'm kissing you slowly while we coast to my room, where I unveil your priceless art by laying you down licking through your curves exploring your town before I spread your legs apart, I said it once, I will say it twice, priceless is what you are and your body is outta sight, as I'm touching you low we begin to blast off into the night like a shooting star, I'm taking your love far, as you soak up my sheets I flip you over and put you on your hands and knees I begin to proceed, sliding in I'm bent at the knees you take a deep breath and breathe, kissing you slowly and gently I am from your neck to your back, I'm going to work, I'm on the attack you're doing the jerk arching that back of yours, so much for you I will endure to explore your passion, turning you around so you can see me in action, putting it down, our tongues lashing as I go deeper screams of you're a keeper comes from you, my legs start to get weaker as I freak you, the King way, the Royal way leaving you speechless with no words to say, doing work pulling a double shift, giving you this special gift late night back breaking legs shaking early morning love making having you moaning loud, scratches to my back as you draw a crowd outside as I push inside right through your eyes I see your soul, this hold I have on you, you could never let go, this is one unbelievable show I'm putting on, my love making comes in different positions, this has been a marathon, I see the white tape, I'm almost at the finish line, we're cruising fast, my love will stay on your mind, you didn't think our bodies would last, it time for us to blast off, at last, you have arrived, you're beautiful river stream down my long, big and thick vine I cum just in time, you sending chills down my spine as my body unwinds, your love was so right, as I take a sip of my wine saying thank you and you're so welcome for attending my **_Formal Invite_** sealing it with a kiss before you hop in your car and drive away deep into the moonlight mist, I will miss you until the next time I can feel your tenderness.

I Can't Explain Your Love

Oh my words aren't enough, when our bodies touch, I knew my love wall would fall down, as soon as I got inside I knew this would be a defining moment in my life, a rush went through my body like a flying rocket as I stroke and hit your pocket kissing and rocking, my feelings are knocking your moans are strong touching my heart like a love song to my ears, taking away my fears to love again, with you I know I will win, touching and kissing, caressing your soft skin as I push within, romance fills the air as pleasure lives in this moment, can't fight, can't hold, my feelings are too bold and strong this love will live on, beyond us, in your love I trust as I thrust and thrust, hard but soft, gentle and smooth smiling from ear to ear are you, shining brighter than the stars at night, you are heaven sent this must be right, our passion's on fire, your intriguing eyes gives me the desire to love you more and take you higher, inspired by your heartbeat in rhythm underneath these sheets, bodies are close, our faces cheek to cheek, whispers of I love you and I feel you deep, keep pushing inside of me I'm about to release, I continue with my creep **I Can't Explain** what you're doing to me, my feelings uncontrollable, a hold I won't let go, going off into the night giving you what you like what you love coming from above, **I Can't Explain** your beautiful love.

Loving You to the Tenth Power

So many thoughts of you being with me, me being with you, all I can see is us in the clouds soaring high to the tenth power you're on my mind every day, every hour, minute and second you keep me guessing, what will you do next, something great I bet, you unbutton my shirt rubbing on my chest kissing at my neck, I pick you up and set you on the computer desk kissing you slowly pulling off your thong inside is where I belong feeling at home when in your throne, flexing while I stroke, (shouts from you) King, you're the best, nevertheless I put you before the rest, next, I pick you giving you all my love as you bounce slow deep I go, laying you on the bed to continue my show, my waves hitting hard rocking your boat, screaming loud as I stroke and stroke, to the tenth Power passion on flames, you're dealing with a real man not no lame, I'm a keep working that thang, you want have no complaints after tonight you won't be the same, making your love rain come down now it's a flood in my town, you're wet, wet calling out this is number one, the best sex I have you flying high to the 10th Power as I work your body through the midnight hours, minute and seconds making you love me every twenty-four/seven.

Just You and Me

I'm on my knees confessing my love to you, crying out for my perfect wife, whom I love everything about, from your head to your feet your smile and pretty teeth, I can see myself with thee for the rest of my life I will say it again and again, I claim you as my wife for in this lifetime I won't let you slip away, forever and now I will stay with you my perfect wife, I love everything that you do I belong to you, the way you kiss me melts my heart when around you I'm in this loving mood, see my heart is yours don't hurt nor break it my soul couldn't take it, forever will I adore thee can't you see you belong to me, heaven sent this love right here is where we are meant to be, never will I bend or fold forever holding on, you're more precious than gold, never breaking this bond to the stars and beyond, creating our own space, our own kingdom where we lay, I'm so happy like a little kid at play time, forever you will be mine just you and me just the two, can't nobody compare to what you do, I will be nothing without you, wouldn't know what to do where to go you have the keys to my heart, mind and soul, igniting my love never letting go forever this love will continue to grow and grow, trusting you with everything that I have, I am glad that it's you who is my better half, one day we will add one bundle of joy, which will make three, raising one happy family **Just you and Me.**

My Masterpiece

I can't hold back my feelings any longer, with you I know I will grow stronger, my love is overflowing burning with everlasting desire and passion for you, with you I know I can conquer all things that are in my path, if anything or anyone gets in the way of my love for you then they will feel my wrath, today I gained an angel, **My Masterpiece,** I am a lucky fellow, I pledge to be the man you need me to be, I vow to love thee, wipe away all tears and fears, no hurt or harm will ever come near, you're dealing with a real man, know that your heart is my precious gift, we are about to embark on a special journey are you ready for this lifetime trip, holding your heart close to me at all times, know that I will forever cherish your love, never will my heart, my love for you perish, I will never give up I love you too much my love, my words are something you can trust, no matter if we fight or fuss your love is a must have in my life, **My Masterpiece**, my wife, the love we share I can't compare it to no one else, I never think twice or question myself when it comes to you, I do question God asking how did He find time to make the perfect woman for me, from the butterscotch lightness of your smooth beautiful skin I knew you were heaven sent from the first time I laid eyes on you, to the hairs on your head silky black and long going down the middle of your back, I'm so glad to call you my own, you love it when I pull on your hair when I'm on the attack, smiling you are when you're looking back at me, even those few wrinkles in your cheeks when you smile drives me crazy and wild inside, I can see right through your beautiful hazel, brown eyes to the depths of your soul I will hold you close never letting you go, to your cute little nose kissing the tip, my eyes are moving to those sexy lips as I step back and take a mental flick of the way you lick your lips, full and thick, moving to your physique having me speaking in a different language, (French) oh oui, oui you got what I need, from those curves you twist and turn around showing that apple bottom, I smile saying wow what have I found, looking at your waist my hearts beats and race, my eyes on those thighs thick and nice just how I like my Queen finally has arrived, even those pretty toes of yours are right, giving you my heart, my all knowing we will go far, beyond the skies past the stars my love shoots past Mars beautiful is what you are, I'm thanking God for sending you to me, you are all I will ever need, my perfect woman, **My Masterpiece**.

True Love

*For so long I been searching for **True Love** to come my way, I just knew you were the right one, you have a glow that outshines the sun, you will come second to none, our hearts are joined together formed as one, your love I can never run from, no more looking for me I am done, I have found my **True Love**, from the very first day I took a vow to stay in your life and make you my wife, without you knowing, my love for you is pouring running over my cup I can't get enough of you my angel from above thanking God for sending me this love, when I look at you I see my Queen, I won't pretend that your beauty doesn't have an effect on me, this is not a dream but reality, your smile is what makes me whole just seeing you brings joy to my soul, the beauty of your loving passion has stolen my heart, I can hardly stand when we are apart, I can no longer keep my love trapped inside my feelings for you I will no longer hide, I'm going outside to scream it from the top of my lungs, world I have found that one, from the first time I laid my eyes on you, my heart just knew that this was **True Love** and I will forever belong to you.*

A Brand New Day

Rest your head on my chest my love and close your eyes, I can guarantee everything will be alright, for when you wake up to the sweet sunrise it will be **A Brand New Day**, with me making sure you feel special in every little way, turning down the lights as I pull you closer I'm feeling the heat of our hearts together like I'm supposed to, on this **Brand New Day** you can tell from the look upon my face, that you're my girl you are my world, this love could never be erased, I will scream that from coast to coast, from place to place, brag and boast I'm pledging to you that I love you the most as we lay for when you awake to the soft morning breeze it will be **A Brand New Day**, but I will continue to love you the same and even more, I will forever explore different ways to please and love you, relaxing your body I am as I run my fingers through your hair caressing as I stare at your beauty, letting all life's worries melt away for when you wake with the feel of a warm summer scent, it will be **A Brand New Day**, falling fast asleep and dreaming with a whisper of I love you passing through my ear, you eliminate all my fears I'm here to stay for when we wake in each other's arms, it will be **A Brand New Day**.

Counting Down the Days

My love, my life, I hate to leave your side, I haven't left yet and I'm already **Counting Down the Days** until the next time I see your face, until the next time I get to touch you below the waist, kiss you and hold your body close to mine, the way your smile lights up the room, your aura just shines, you can change any bad mood into a good groove, just thinking about you give me chills down my spine, one fact I know, I love you deep down to my soul, every little touch makes me feel whole, rich, on top of the world with you being my girl my Queen, my everything to me, you are who I need when I'm away from you at work or at home sitting alone it's you I think of, you controlling my thoughts, closing my eyes wishing I can open my window and fly to you under the moonlight, I will fight for your love that is one of a kind, I'm **Counting Down the Days** until I make you mine, in due time you will find yourself back in my arms, to know surprise loving my embrace feeling and knowing that you're safe, no matter what may come our way, in any shape or form I won't allow any harm to come to you, protecting you I will, fulfilling your every need I'm blessed with skills, these actions I take are real, protecting your heart with my shield I'm **Counting Down the Days** until I feel your love again, you complete from within.

Imagine

Can you handle King if he goes there with you?, putting you in that natural groove, you will feel every move in all that I do, If you feel you can, then step up to the plate, today may be your lucky day as we play this baseball game I say, your body has become my mound, I hope you can handle what I pitch, trust in me I will have that body in a twist, heart full of love, I will have you feeling like you're flying high like a dove, your eyes filled with tears of joy, your soul on fire with the ignition of my love, then you will see that we go hand and hand like a glove, an angel is what you are, my shooting star we going deep, I'm taking you far, stay in my world baby, beautiful is what you are, let me take this to the next level, I'll never let you go this is a show worth paying for as I stroke your core kissing you soft and gentle, while you're adoring the passion it's a lot of back and forth action, seeing satisfaction across your face as I go low in between your waist, giving you a little taste in that right place, opening up that flow down your palace, just close your eyes and **Imagine** if 'King was doing this to your palace, could you handle., could you **Imagine**?

My Twelve Royal Ways

*Sit back and get ready for a ride, tonight you will experience **My Twelve Royal Ways** turning you into my sex slave as I get ready to have that body blazing and misbehaving, you will forever crave me after this show, here we go, One, interlocking our hands guiding you into my kingdom of love there's nothing to be scared of, two, as I sit you down moving over to the bar while taking off my crown, grabbing two glasses four ice cubes two in each glass, I subtract, Ciroc on the rocks is how I drink love, I see you're a straight shooter I'm pouring in your glass no ice tonight is a one of a kind night, I have you on fire like a gun this party has just begun, I will show you that I am the best thing under the sun, I hold up the number three as you come stand next to me, whispers of sex me King as I grab you with the look of ecstasy in my eyes your passion can't hide, kissing your lips sending a chill through your hips, you're touching and rubbing feeling that I'm well equipped with your thighs passion is in your eyes, I lay you on the floor by the fireplace, welcome to that sweet number four, your body I'm about to explore, looking at how your body glows off the flames of my fire I'm about to fulfill your every desire, you smile with a sexy look upon your face unbuckling my pants giving you a little dance with my lips to your lips, to your neck from your neck my tongue goes down the middle of your breasts as I caress you feeling so wet, you're loving my kisses, you haven't felt nothing yet, wait until you feel my* sex, hooking your thighs in between my arms I see it's time for number five as I stand up to perform, I'm nothing like the norm, you're screaming you like my form, you're feeling so warm, you're loving my Royal stick as we move to number six, this is a King's mix turning you around hooking your thighs onto my thighs backwards as I slide you ride, I'm feeling your passion from deep inside the number seven is in sight, you're loving my might my power, giving you what you desire my beautiful flower, I'm going deeper into your heaven, it's time to devour, going low I haven't eaten, well what do you know its lucky number eight, I pleasure your palace better than your wildest dreams deeper than what you can image, coming up with that sticky face loving your taste licking you up and down until you say stop, I have you running like you're a robber and I'm a cop, making your palace pop as I lick that spot and that spot in between where it's warm and hot, coming up top to rock your spot, turning you around here comes the number nine as I get behind giving you all my love, we're going higher than the clouds laying it down all night, you saying nine is just right flowing all over my sheets your knees, legs are weak, we're almost to that number ten, no doubt you are about to cum again and again, I continue to keep your head, your feelings on spin, moving on to number eleven, where you're bound to win, you're loving this time I spent going deeper into your heaven just like number seven, eleven gave you more chills, there's no more doubts in your mind about my skills, I have almost fulfilled my dozen, your juice box is hotter than an oven, I'm showing you nothing, but good loving the way I've dealt with your body, number twelve is the end of the party, but nevertheless it will have you on melt, for my next trick will make you never want anybody else, I pick you up, I have your body on tilt you wrap your hands around the back of my neck as I kiss and pull on your bottom lip, you begin to bounce up and down as I dip in between your hips, you feel me shift into another gear while nibbling on your ear, **My Twelve Royal Ways** are nothing you will have to fear even after we are long done, when you think about **My Twelve Royal Ways** you will scream out King is number one, you are the only man I want under the sun, this is what you will feel, each and every time I deal **My Twelve Royal Ways** turning you into my love slave.

One Night

Making true love is all you want to do, you've been looking for a real love all your life, even if it's just for **One Night**, my loving will consume your dreams for the rest of your life, If you had **One Night** with me, it will be better than your fantasy, because I am reality, I will do nothing, but please when down in between, making you love me forever, grabbing your legs and bending you at the knees, touching with my tongue giving your body what it needs, taking over your world, turning you into a woman, from a girl, when I lick and play with your pearl, afraid you don't have to be this is real love and ecstasy, my music on slow, as I turn the lights down low, lighting candles so you can see me handle that body of yours, tonight you will score, I am what you been looking for, giving you what your body deserves, I came from heaven to your earth to show you what your worth, as I go to work blowing your mind, not here to waste your time, that pretty face of yours is so fine, your beauty is so divine, I will cross rivers and climb mountains while fighting off lions, just to see you my jewel, my pretty diamond, as I stroke your body taking you far, this love is not blinded, so pure you are, you never been touched feeling a rush through your body you can't hold it in, you can't fight it, your soul has been ignited with not lust, but my love fitting tight like some gloves, my sweet dove from above, I'm your eagle soaring high, but low as I go in between those thighs getting you right, your *body temperature on the rise and rising, to no surprise your flow begins to stream down your thighs, glancing up into your eyes loving this* **One Night** *as I slide back into your cave of passion, we're lip locking with a lot of tongue lashing, you're feeling every thrust and every actions, pulling my hips closer when I stroke, it's like waves crashing against a boat, doing circles as I stroke, whispers from me of can you keep up with King? Standing tall as I slide around and around bringing your love walls down, you're dealing with a real man no clown, as I spread your love apart and start to pound pulling your hair turning your face around, I'm seeing nothing, but smiles while I explore your town, you're throwing it back as I arch your back, you're holding on to the bed post tightly, loving my attack, as I thrust with all my might giving it to you right on this* **One Night**, *in the middle of your love, you can't get enough as you bust and bust, I see nothing, but trust in your closing eyes, falling asleep in my arms into the sunrise, waking up to find a note by your side, leaving you with the thoughts of our* **One Night**.

Undying Love

The first time I saw you my heart began to pound, not even knowing what I had found, hoping and wishing one day you will wear my crown that has yet to be given away, every Wednesday night I will get a sight, a glimpse of you and sometimes we just might drop a line or two, you're not even knowing that I was so into you, each time you will sing you make my heart move, those are just a few little things that made me have **Undying Love** for you, so beautiful you are, every Sunday morning until the evening I got to be in your presence, you were always shining bright like a star, a gift is what you are sent straight from heaven, without question I will always be here for you, for so long I've wanted to be with you and have you in my life, way back then I knew I wanted you as my wife, to hold and to love, I want you to know that I cared about you so much, wishing, but never have I felt your touch, I want to show you my love is something you can trust, you are the one, my one, my ever wonder what if, that would have been a crazy twist, I must admit people would have blown their tip, you are a special gift there should be rose petals thrown at your feet, allow me to take your love on a trip, your smile is so innocent and sweet, seeing you brings a joy to my soul, your love has taken over me, you stole my heart and don't even know it happen a long time ago as a teen, now grown and still my heart has an **Undying Love** for you, it sweeps me off my feet, I kept the love I have for you in a secret place, I kept it safe, waiting for that one special day you used the key and unveiled the love that I have inside of me for you, my love hasn't gone anywhere, it's the reason why all my relationships have failed, can't you tell, without you I'm in hell, like a prisoner in jail waiting on bail, no matter how much time has gone by I know this what failed, I can't lie, there's an **Undying Love** I hold inside for you my love flies past the moon, past the stars I will follow you to Mars that's how fine you are, even to Venice, where women are the meanest, it doesn't matter because of what I'm feeling, love, I will go to the end of the earth if I knew I had a shot at showing you what my love is worth, it's not just about what you have under your shirt, there's a connection, an attraction, that we both have been having, it's time we become one and make it happen, inside my heart your love equals my satisfaction, my love will never grow old or fold, it's time I take action, this love is true I will always have an **Undying Love** for you.

Lost Love

I should have been loving you when I had the chance, when you were my woman and I was your man, now I can't stand being away from you, I miss the things we used to do, since I have been without you it's been so hard to play the part with another, this one, that one, in and out my covers, that one this one only to discover, they couldn't match or come close to the things you could do, you were my true Queen, see what I mean, it dates back to those kid days crushing on you, no one knew I had deep love for you, keeping my feelings on the low, waiting for the right day and time I could reveal my feelings and let my love show, together our love would just flow, float on a cloud, sending chills up and down each other's spines each and every time our hands and bodies became entwined, when I used to look through your sexy brown eyes I could see your heart with mine, I fast forward to us being older reconnecting on one special new year's night, not kids anymore your body I did finally explore, leaving an lasting endeavor impression on your mind, I had you already thinking about the next time you will become mine, passing through the years, so much time has gone by, but it's you I think of when I'm alone at home in my bed at night, no matter what was going on in our lives we stayed in contact, with so much passion for you deep down inside, showing you where my heart is at, loving you for life is a known fact, I'm letting you know I'm coming back home via text get ready for the best sex, the best night of your life, finally home and it's you I'm calling on my phone telling you I'm ready for you I'm where you belong, for tonight I cannot be alone, you fly over like the road runner it's time for me to uncover this passion I once felt before, how you're making me feel inside while I'm pushing inside is nothing I want to hide anymore, your love, your heart I do adore, I'm ready to take you to that next level, I'm digging six feet and deeper with my love shovel, not caring if the world knows, in any case my love for you it shows, remember when we were on that dark road, oh how you let your love go, giving me that Queen show, your lips, your hips, those thighs kept me on rise, at any given time you was ready always catching me by surprise, I love it when I look into your eyes, I see my life, my soul, my wife who makes me whole, never could I get enough, never am I letting go of my **Lost Love***.*

Take My Time

Back again for the first time, I felt like I never left the way you still blow my mind, with every touch that's so divine having my thoughts, my body in a twist as I **Take My Time** and do you right, I have you in full take off at first sight, I love our time, each time giving you what you need, when you come and be with me, your mind, body and soul everything you may hold, I cherish to the bone, damn I love to hear you moan when I'm touching you, calling my name in that chilled tone, making me go harder stroking long and deep giving you all of me, as I rock your body all over my throne, scratches, screams and moans is the song being played through your body as I push inside, enjoying the ride you are by far my shooting star kissing and touching, pushing on with this journey **Taking My Time**, not forgetting this present is a gift, making love to you like this is the last time, kissing your body soft and gentle, you're so fine, beautiful you are I say as I stroke loving you like I will never see you again as we coast, never will I finish this loving making is never ending, as I **Take My Time** thirsting for your body like fine wine, I'm nominating you because I only want you, showing you how my love groove as I push inside of you kissing your neck you haven't felt nothing yet, my heart belongs to you it's nothing I won't do to prove that I'm feeling you, lighting up my day and changing my bad moods just me and you, standing you up as I give you a thrust, your body erupts with passion, I'm giving that ass a *good thrashing no time for relaxing, watch my actions as we move slow rocking as we float you're my sea and I'm your boat, coasting and exploring until I hit shore, loving the night away, giving you more as we lay, giving you all of me blessing you on this lovely day, making you weak in the knees as I proceed, holding you tightly as my arms enfolds you close, doing the most, feeling all between your walls our love has evolved, another night falls, two days have passed and our love making is still lasting, no need to speed up and go fast, I am your teacher welcome to my class, it's up to me if you will pass, so far I am glad, but pay attention so you will outlast the rest, keep hitting me with that natural high, show me why you are the best, now I'm faded off you, my love I need your drug,* **Taking My Time** *with your love as I erupt like a volcano, to you, your love I can never say no, as our this love making will last a lifetime... (To be continued).*

Up All Night

Tossing and turning has me **Up All Night**, thinking of you my girl and the way we make love is out of this world, you just don't know what you do to me, let me break it down so you can forever see what you mean to me, you have me flying around high in the sky, free as a bird floating and coasting over the earth, I can't lie, your body is so banging so right, every time I look through your gorgeous eyes, you have my heart pumping and escalating, taking flight, your beauty is out of sight, blowing my mind each time I'm graced with your presence I feel I'm getting a piece of heaven here on earth, I'm **Up All Night** thinking about you and knowing your worth with every passing second there will be no replacing of you and the things you do, I'm loving our sex giving it to you the best I am, what's next, me being surprised by you creeping into my room and climbing into my sheets, I see we're on to a different horizon as I slide in gripping your thighs, kissing you slow while pushing inside, you never felt this way before in your life, your love is about to explode, you're ready to become my wife the way I do your body, you just might have to miss your class in the morning due to us being **Up All Night**, you're loving my mental as well, the mind I possess keeps you guessing taking away all your stress this love is one of a kind, you are blessed, never have before you laid eyes on a man that you can adore for the rest of your life, my love for you comes deep from within my core past my soul, it's you, your love that is making me feel whole and complete, we're not even finished yet and I can't wait for the next time you come sneaking, climbing into my sheets showing me how freaky you can be, I'm making sure with every stroke you feel me deep, your smile your love is so sweet, all this time I was dreaming of you being with me, not knowing I must have fallen back to sleep, if only you were lying next to me so I can show you how much you mean to me, with my actions I will be showing you how much love lives inside of me, satisfaction is guaranteed, thanking God above for the heart you share, I will always keep you near never will I stray away from your love, you are my gift, you have granted my one special wish, I love it when we kiss, our passion is filled with so much bliss, your love I can't dismiss, never can I resist, I'm attaching my heart with yours tonight I will explore and adore your love for life, it's so hard to sleep, I need you next to me, until it's your eyes I see, I will be **Up All Night** thinking about the day you will become my wife.

Pleasure

*I want you to sit back, relax and allow King to show you the way to everlasting **Pleasure**, baby follow the road signs to my world, rest assured once you step inside this **Pleasure** you will forever want to be my girl, my love making you can't compare, I'm going to make your toes curl once I enter your palace, you will feel like you are floating high in the air, I will kiss you everywhere yes even there in that warm spot as I hold you close the way I kiss and stroke licking on your neck before I rock your boat, that's just a taste of what I can do once I begin to indulge in your body, my **Pleasure** can't be measured you won't fight it, I promise I won't leave you dissatisfied, come in and take my hand let King guide you to lovers' land, laying you on the bed kissing you so soft, running my fingers through your hair hope you are prepared, as I raise you up into a chair position we're still lip locking and tongue twisting, pleasuring your body is my mission, while I'm taking off your shirt and popping your bra, we still kissing ever so softly, I flip you over and begin to kiss your shoulders, down your back, playing with your freaky emotions rubbing you down with this hot oil lotion, now I see I have your feelings in motion, sending **Pleasure** down your body with my hands, like I said I hope you prepare as I take you there, ecstasy is where we will be going, you put that sexy arch in your back as I spread you low licking you slowly, you starting to glaze you starting to flow as I lick you* low this is a King **Pleasure** show, a star I am out shining the rest this I know, you've never been to a show like this before, rising up I am to push in slow, making sure you feel every inch, every stroke, I'm going deep where no light can creep you're clinching and grabbing the sheets face in my pillow as you let out a scream, I turn you over so I can get in between those thighs, through your eyes I can tell this is the best night of your life, as I **Pleasure** your body inside and out I feel your body climaxing with nails in my back as you scream and shout, exploding pulling me close holding me tight you are, squeezing me with those thighs as my **Pleasure** begins to rise ever so high, you can't fight King's power, I can love you for hours, days and months, your body I'm devouring with my passion giving that ass a good thrashing maxing out, I have you taping out down for the count, my **Pleasure**, my love will never wear out, lasting forever without a doubt my **Pleasure** will have you hotter than the desert, when I'm pushing down south, my **Pleasure** can't be measured, the word love will roll from your mouth, showing you in many different ways and forms what my love is about, exceeding all your expectations in giving you **Pleasure** without a doubt.

Falling in Love

These last few weeks have been very special to me, being with you spending time with you has me **Falling in Love** with you, igniting a love that was locked away deep down lost and couldn't be found like buried treasure, your every smile your every touch I cannot measure your kiss so soft and gentle, you have my mental **Falling** in thoughts of you when we are apart, when we are together it's priceless art, your sweet conversation the words you speak I cherish those sexy lips of yours they make me weak, you are my fetish I'm **Falling** uncontrollably my emotions are getting the best of me, whatever you are doing baby don't stop there's no denying me, I need you next to me, you are everything to me, your beauty is the reason why I breathe, you're so fine I'm caught up in your web like a fly waiting for you to arrive so I can give you a surprise as I look into your eyes I can see your soul, I don't want half of you, I want you as a whole this love I can't let go, never will we break never will I escape the feeling of me **Falling in Love** with you, these words I will forever say, no one can ever take your place, I will love you until my final resting day.

Beyond the Clouds

You are my one and only your love equals my heart, this love is flying amongst the stars, **Beyond the Clouds**, do you know how beautiful you are, I say it with a smile as I proceed to lay your body down on Mars, you stay shining brighter than every star lighting up the sky like it's daytime, you're grabbing at my milky way as I start to climb on top and take center stage to show you what I've got, well-endowed and I'm not a minute man, you have no words to say speechless as I begin to rock the sheets giving you all my loving, you're scratching my back and grabbing my cheeks pulling me tight so I can go deeper inside, kissing you everywhere while my hands rub against your thighs, yes even there my tongue will raise you high, this love you will not want to share, keeping you flying **Beyond the Clouds** bringing your love all the way down, showing you I'm not fooling around, I don't play when it comes to my love making, they call me the great, I will have your feelings in a different place, a different space, **Beyond the Clouds** this love you could never erase or replace, having you hot not mild, with your love running free and wild, each time I take you **Beyond the Clouds**.

Never Ending

Tonight is the night, Tell your girls you're not coming out tonight your King is about to take you for a ride, go to the backroom I have it fixed up right, rose pedals everywhere, coconut candlelight scents light up the room and fill the air, your mouth drops as you stop and stare turning around throwing your arms in the air, wrapping them around my neck into my eyes you stare, kissing you slowly telling you to tie up your hair and get ready for a show, as I pour us a drink plus a shot ready to show you how I'm going to make your body rock, that **Never Ending** love going all night, I'm going to pop that body right, I will have you on a natural high flying to the moon with the things I do, on a **Never Ending** journey when I'm inside you, your love, until the day I die and even then our souls will reach on high beyond the skies, true love never dies nor lies, look into my eyes and feel my heart know that it's yours for you are my choice, I will scream it loud over any crowd so the world hears my voice, this love is **Never Ending**, this is the start of a new beginning, with you I am winning, this love could never be finished.

A Love Groove Called You

Loving the way these candles are bringing out the beauty in your skin, making a move doing what I do once you step into my room, you're feeling so good too good for it to be a sin, loving the way you sound when you allow me in, a fool for your **Love Groove**, kissing you showing you my moves, pulling your G-string down taking it off, rubbing your body you're feeling so feather soft, I can't get enough of you, the more I get the more I want to be inside of your **Love Groove**, giving you what's yours, King's body is here for you to explore have no fear because ecstasy is near, fulfilling all your fantasies bringing them to reality, satisfaction guaranteed, indeed I'm everlasting, loving your smile your style outshines any other, my sexy freak under covers, loving me like no other, I'm giving it to you, this is all for you, just us two, I'm **Loving this Groove Called You.**

All I Ever Wanted

Becoming a part of your heart, your life is **All I Ever Wanted,** for us to be together, for us to never be apart, to fight through any stormy weather, my battle for your love goes far, I will climb any mountain, swim any seas no one in this world compares to thee, to you my love this is true, you're perfect and so is this love we share, we have so much more than I ever thought we would, I love you more than I ever thought I could, I promise to give you all I have to give, I'll do anything for you for as long as I live, in your beautiful eyes I see our present and I see our future, thanking my past, by the way you look at me I know this will last, unlike the last, I know you are the one, when seen through my eyes, my heart, my soul never lies, you are my Queen my Wife **All I Ever Wanted** in my life.

Drunken Night

*Rolling around up and down in this bed, look at what this drinking has led us to do, just you and me this was meant to be, or did we have too much to drink? Whatever the case maybe, through my eyes I see your heart beats to the rhythm of me, my groove loving the way your hips move as we go higher than the moon, lips so soft and smooth as we kiss and kiss I grab your thighs and hips, I raise you high to the sky as I push inside your palace, looking in your eyes kissing while you bounce slow deep and long strokes, shut your eyes and imagine King doing his thing, making you feel like a Queen by any means I will do anything to please your soul, as I go stroke by stroke with my tongue, you scream out I'm about to cum holding tight squeezing with all your might, shaking and everything making you fiend as that cream stream down your walls, number one I am called the way I slide through your halls, busting like a loaded gun showing you how royalty is done on this **Drunken Night**, hitting you hard with my pipe, as tears falls from your eyes, but it is a joyous cry, never have you felt this way inside as I push inside giving it to you just right until the morning sunlight intrude waking up like what just happened? Kim, is that you? Looking for our clothes saying tell me we didn't do these actions, how did we get from the party to this room, phone is ringing and it's you, what am I to do...(To be continued).*

My Mind's Screaming Out

My Mind's Screaming Out make love to me, my body **Screaming Out** feed your love to me, give me everything, you are what I need, no words, just my thoughts, the way you touch, lick and kiss makes me adore as I take an adventure through your core, touching me in places my body thought had lost feelings, with passion and desire not lust, but love might I mention, loving your sexually healing giving me just what I want from the top of my head to the tip of my toes loving the way you explore more and more, giving me a sensational rush making all my tiny hairs stand up by just one touch from you, **My Mind's Screaming Out** what will I do if I didn't have you, would I feel what I feel, you came into my life and revealed true love to me, healed my heart from being cold, now hot and warm I will forever hold, my love for you I will forever show, forever prove my worthiness, I miss your lips and kiss, I love it when our tongues twist, your love I cannot resist, like a closed fist I'm holding onto you with a tight grip, this is no movie, I have no script, my heart is my gift to you, **My Mind's Screaming Out** I love everything about you, my heart and love will forever be closed and sealed if it weren't for you coming into my life showing me that this love is just right, making me whole, making me feel that love is real with bringing joy to my soul, alone I will be without you in my home next to me.

Come See Me

*Calling to see what's your plans for the night, asking if you would like to **Come See Me** and be with King for the night, letting you know I need you as bad as a heartbeat, I want to hear you scream through the night, baby come fulfill my fantasy please, but you had a million and one excuses why you couldn't **Come See Me** and test my jets, you know take flight unto the sunset, now I'm feeling down and hurt by your reject, a little anger is building, I'm feeling upset, with this drink in my hand trying to figure out how to get, my love here with me tonight, little did I know you were on your way to give me a Queen show, my doorbell rings, to myself I'm thinking who could it be, I don't want to deal with anyone right now besides my Queen, I proceed to opening up the door, to my surprise it's you standing there looking all fly in your heels with your trench coat on, pulling you close to me is where you belong, embracing your warm comfort while speaking in your ear, saying you pulled a fast one on me I didn't know you were near, what if I had another woman in here, with a laugh as you push me back we took one look into each other's eyes with me saying no you're my match, I want no one, but you at my side, moving in closer to each other's lips, to give a passionate kiss, as the fire rise, I pick you up kicking the door shut carrying you through the living room to my bedroom of love, gently while we're still kissing I lay you on my bed, where passion and love is about to be given, I* start to unbutton your jacket only to find nothing, but lace everything underneath, kissing every inch of your body not leaving any part untouched, I will lick you clean, looking you in your eyes you're telling me how you love me so much, I responded with I love you more and kiss your lips, my love it's you I adore placing my hand in between your hips, my fingers begin to take a dip not surprised at how wet you are I have your body shooting off like a star on a nice flow as I gently enter your passion beginning to stroke you up with my back and forth action, holding each other tight I'm not extending far, oh how beautiful you are, splashing your juices all over me, I love the way I feel when inside, by the smile on your face I see you agree, giving you all of me, showing you I am a need in your life, nobody else will be able to lay pipe down quite as nice like me, our rhythm is in sync to one another, flipping you over as you bust on my covers, I start to go harder, but gently as my hands glide down your back, you about to fall in love with my attack, beginning to call my name you are, moaning louder and louder, I'm going deeper and further with each stroke my love invokes thee, you have a spell over me, each time you show me why you complete me, I love you deeply, blessed I am when you **Come to See Me.**

My Player Bone is Gone

*King has it going on with me is where you belong, my **Player Bone is Gone**, exceeded all my wrongs, this is my last song, my last chance, maybe my last dance, I have to get back to you before our love is dead, going round and round thinking of ways to get you back, take you from that clown you belong in my town the Queen of my world my woman my girl, wiping away those frowns all smiles when I come around, you never forgot the way I lay your body down, I'm the King of my castle and want you to be the Queen of my palace, imagine us two, there's nothing we won't be able to do, you're wanting more and more so I give it to you without stopping me busting is not an option, giving you that ultimate satisfaction, so much fire and passion inside of me you don't know what to do with me, finally giving you what you always asked of me what you deserve for you to be my only girl, my only woman, for you I am coming no more running, I'm ready to give you one hundred plus, your love is a must, time and time again this topic was discussed, for you my **Player Bone is Gone**, let's build on trust.*

Rejection

The day has come that I thought would never exist, **Rejection** feels like being cut low, will my heart ever be fixed? this girl had it all, slim at the waist, pretty in the face, thick in the hips with some nice round full lips, baby had me floating on tilt, she's not to short, but not too tall either just right and I had to meet her, I thought she could be the one, bad as hell and hotter than a smoking gun, every guy that stepped to her has been turned down like a thumb, I could see myself with no one but her, quiet as kept, I am the next big thing under the sun, let's see if she loves me for me before my riches and fame come, her face looks as soft as fur everything else around me is a blur I see nothing or no one besides her, but will she go for a guy like me who isn't showing off, popping bottle and flashing money or will she see me for who I am and become my honey? The night isn't getting any younger I walk over smile and greet her with a gentle shake and kiss to the hand as I say, pleased to meet you can I buy you a drink or two, she takes one look at me like you're not my type shoo!, flee get away from me, my brow begins to frown walking away in disbelief how can somebody so fine be so ugly, when she doesn't even know me, she didn't even give me chance, don't know what type of plans I had unfolding in my hands, not knowing I was getting ready to sign a check for millions, years pass by and I became a new guy, money falling from the sky, drop top Mercedes Benz when I ride, same club different time, who spots me, that fine wine by no surprise her eyes are big, wide and bright, but I still remember how cruel she was that night, now she wants to see what life will be like if she became my wife, sike, when I reply, when you had the chance you dismissed me when you didn't even know my plan, that same year I was given an advance on my book, trips to London and Paris now you looking all shook, I knew this day would happen, I knew it would come, this was meant for me to look you in the eyes and say the same thing you said to me on the unforgettable night, shoo!, flee you're not my type get away from me, can't you see I'm looking for a real woman who's not turned on by the money she sees, but one who's turned on by my touch, the way I look into her eyes and how our hearts coincide with each pump I feel inside the love we will share for the rest of our lives, those were the words I used when I chose to reply.

Borrowed Time

Texting and calling when we can be on **Borrowed Time**, having to plan carefully so you don't get caught by your man, you belong to another hand, but with the way I crept into your forbidden land I have you ready to leave your man, having you creeping around town, there's so much joy when we come around each other, looking like we're some undercover spies as we meet up on this cold and rainy night, for only one night out of the week I fulfill your passion your fantasy, setting your soul on fire, filling every one of your desires, all night long for hours of pleasure on this **Borrowed Time**, throughout the week your man can't measure up to the way I do your body when I pull inside it, in my mind it's you I seek your love I want next to me every day of the week, your man can't compete with the way I groove, I have all the right tools when inside between your thighs, I stay having your body on a different type of temperature as I rise to the occasion, my royal begins his invasion blowing up your spot, making you hotter than hot, but cool when I kiss, you are loving the way I move, I'm just giving you a taste as I pull out to go below your waist with my tongue as we lay forgetting about tomorrow, but knowing it will come knowing we're on **Borrowed Time**, I flip you over and continue to lick down your spine as your body begins to unwind, so sexy, so fine you are, I cherish these moments I know every socket every component on your body, I study for your thang, you're going to pass me with honors, handing out recommendations the way I have you screaming when we're love making, back breaking exchanging sex faces on **Borrowed Time**, he could never hold your body tight like I do, close as we coast, me rocking your boat, kissing you slowly so soft and genuine I can't pretend I don't love when I'm within your fire I look forward to our one night all night doing you just right, every week I bring you to your knees, are you ready to leave and move in with me, you're starting to fall in love I can see on **Borrowed Time** for just one night I make sure you see your worth, greatest gift God ever created here on earth, I have your body going crazy, going berserk as it's almost my time to clock out and get off work, raising your leg high as I go deeper inside your body climaxing, thrashing with passion, you're raining down my pipe line we're exploding at the same damn time on this **Borrowed Time**, your heart will forever belong with mine.

Our Love

This love was destined to be, you and me, my heart is filled with love, never thought it could be done, you have me so ready to see you walk down that aisle, meeting you at the altar seeing that smile, my feelings going wild inside, you're the ultimate high, dreams coming true who are you?, my angel, my love, my Queen, me?, your world, your everything your King, expressing what I mean each and every day, I know your worth, your value to the tenth power our loving will conquer and devour anything in its path, we are destined to last so thankful for our past, the others didn't know what they had, glad you do, **Our Love** goes down to the roots, growing strong never will we ever be alone again this love is blessed from the man above, without sin, no devil you can't corrupt **Our Love**, you want win, this is special like never catching a unicorn the way **Our Love** forms a strong bond, this love is for sure to live on like a Michael Jackson song, even when we are dead and gone, are souls will carry **Our Love** up high, these feelings are just so right, so blessed to have you in my life, you becoming my wife for all time I don't mind, because Our type of Love is hard to find.

Without You

You bring stability to my life, you're so beautiful I will cherish you for life, I wouldn't know what to do if I couldn't call you my wife, this is how I will feel if I couldn't have you near, **Without You** I'm as hopeless as a penny with a hole in it, you won't be able to spend it, tossing it to the gutter where I will be living the rest of my days until I can be saved, my mind constantly spinning and spinning **Without You** in my life I will be through, done for, I wouldn't have anything to live for, your love, your body, mind and soul I do adore, never taking your love for granted, just the thought of being **Without You** I can't stand it, I don't want to even imagine so much passion lives inside of me for you, sometimes it brings me down to my knees, yes I get weak when I think of you not being with me, my love open your eyes and see **Without You** I wouldn't know what to do, **Without You** I couldn't breathe, feels as if I'm suffocating, gasping as you disappear right before my eyes in thin air, your love I can never compare to another, at night I will sleep on your side holding your pillow and favorite blanket, I couldn't make it without your love making, your body so fine when you standing there in your birthday suit, naked baby I'm not faking **Without You** my body be aching, **Without You** I'm lost like a son without a mother, rain and thunder, pain and hurt is all I will feel wishing it was a dream and not reality, **Without You** I cannot eat, body not allowing food to digest, because your heart no longer beats inside my chest, my mind, heart and soul will be a mess, **Without You** I get no rest, can't even sleep, means I want die, I will be trapped on this earth forever, for life, **Without You** by my side to look me in my eyes to tell me everything will be alright, these feelings I cannot hide, without your touch I won't feel alive, more like a ghost feeling cold, mad at the world because it's you I want to hold, smell, feel and see, you mean everything to me, my love runs deeper than all the blue seas, shines brighter than the sun, I'm nominating you as my number one, **Without You** I am no one, alone I will be with no one to call my own, I need you to sit beside my throne, for all time our love will reach higher than high, **Without You** my skies won't be big and blue, but dark and grey because I am **Without You** this is true the way I will feel if I didn't have you near each and every day.

My Beautiful Find

Seeing you takes me back in time, calling you **My Beautiful Find,** I remember when I was seven I saw a piece of heaven on earth, an angel arose from the dirt, since then I knew your worth, when I became nine I never thought I would come to find you again, even then this love for you starts to begin, starts to form, as I would watch you cheer and perform at the basketball games too shy to walk up and ask your name, back to heaven when I turned eleven, I love to be in your presence, you not knowing how I feel for you, this love I know it's true, it's real I can feel it deep down in my soul, you have a hold on me that I can never let go, **My Beautiful Find** I always felt in my heart that you were mine, waiting for the right time I can pursue and make you mine, in due time your body will become mine, your soul will forever be kept with mine, this love we can share, we will intertwine our hearts tied tight into a knot, so that we will never part, give me a chance and I will show you that we can go far, never have I felt your warm embrace, but I can't tell from the beauty in your face and the way those hips shake that your love is the place I want to be, until the end of time your heart will belong to me, **My Beautiful Find**, in due time... (To be continued..)

All Alone

I never thought this day would appear, me walking into my kingdom and you're no longer here, leaving me alone with an apology note saying you just couldn't do it anymore, I'm running off to explore the seven seas there's no need for you to wait for me I'll find another to worship me, balling up the paper and throwing it further than my eyes can see, galloping on my horse catching you before you set sail, my heart is burning, my eyes are watering, my mouth is screams out say it's not so, tell me my love that you are not about to really leave me **All Alone** *with nobody, but me sitting on the throne, yes it's true my King I have to follow my dream kissing me on the cheek I say wait let me say this one last thing before we say goodbye, wiping my eyes from the weep, these next words I speak I want you to feel it because this is what my heart means to me, I am strong and will have to be this love of mine you will never see and I will never allow for me to feel this weak again, I thought our journey was at the beginning of the start line, but I see we're already at the end of the race from the look upon your face, I'm closing this chapter, stopping the chase, my heart has been locked you choose another to replace where I lay, to love, to hold, I don't need a girl to call my own, I need a woman to sit beside my throne, a real Queen to call my own never will she steer me or do me wrong or leave a note telling me I'm leaving you* **All Alone**, *so don't call my phone once your other man does* what you have done to me and leave you alone, know that you can't come back home, for this palace doesn't belong to you anymore, another will take your place and adore the way I love her with grace, never will I forsake her, won't do anything, but please her with this exceptional love over and over again, in my world in my mind you don't exist anymore, you don't deserve my crown, you are never to return, even step foot in my town, at your very sight I will release the hounds, you didn't have any mercy when you cheated on me so why should I, no more tears drop from my eyes, you're the type of woman I despise, when you have a great man by your side you don't know how to keep him in your life, it's there in clear air I was sharing my wife, you gave away my crown, I'm lost, but will be found, I was Ray Charles to the nonsense, blind and couldn't see what you were doing to me, as you snuck out at night while I was asleep, even when I was on business trips you were away with him locking lips not thinking about me, about how I may feel, your love was never real, from day one I have been in this relationship, my love took off like a spaceship, now I'm back on the same ship in the same boat, **All Alone** by myself now with no one to sit beside my throne.

Deep Inside

All you have to do is tell me how you want it, I'm at your service, your wish is my every command, as we lay right here on this fresh white sand, waves crashing the beach as you lay on top of me, kissing me softly and sweet, my hands stroking your hair passion is in the air, stars filling the skies for tonight is your night, I'm going to take your body for a royal ride, can I go **Deep, Deep Inside** of your love, trying to go Deep in your core, your body I adore, my beautiful angel sent from above, let me go **Deep, Deep Inside** your love, you feel so good on top riding my eagle, as we make love into the night, we are going to need a sequel, the sky is not the limit going longer than a minute, than an hour your body I will devour, this fire, our passion your body I desire, taking you higher than before as we switch positions kissing and touching, going deep into your tomb, you consuming all I do, loving the way I make love to you under the stars, I can still tell how fine you are, gazing into those beautiful eyes as I dip inside, this feeling is so right I can't lie you have my body tied up tonight, while I go **Deep, Deep Inside** sliding in and out between those thighs, I have you singing to the clouds flying high as I begin to raise your thighs onto my shoulders now I'm **Deeper Inside** your love becoming your drug, you becoming my fiend giving you what you need each and every time you call me, making you scream my name, you not giving no complaints the way I have your body in a groove, in this mood called King, I aim to please when you're lying next to me, will have you weak in your knees feeling that quake as you shake, I can't wait to bring your love down, not caring about the people walking around, we are in our world just King and his Queen who means everything to me, you're begging me please don't leave my side we can go all night, achieve what you need as I go **Deep, Deep Inside** giving that body of yours that flow like a river, King always delivers not once, not twice, but for life, you're asking to be my wife, I answer that request while I work you with finesse, we have this beach our sheets are a mess, this was the ultimate test as we lay to rest you fall asleep on my chest, knowing this love is the greatest, it's the best.

Just to See You Again

I will do anything for this woman, there is nothing I wouldn't do **Just To See You Again**, I will swim the deep blue seas if I knew you were waiting at the bottom for me, there's no obstacle to tall, through the hot sandy desert I will crawl, drown in my sweat, hungry and all I will find you even when night falls, **Just To See You Again**, if only for one second I can see that smile again it will last me a lifetime, burning my soul from within, with the passion of your fire taking me higher, **Just To See You Again** I will fly to the sky, to the moon I only have eyes for you, this love I know this is true, I will take any route **Just To See You Again**, with you by my side I'm bound to win, there is no pretend in this love, all real sent from heaven above, precious you are the most beautiful thing I have seen by far, anywhere you are I will go far for you to the end of the world my girl, **Just To See You Again** I will spend my last, never will I ever pass up an opportunity a moment to be with you, this love is true, my heart, mind, body and soul belongs to you.

Wanting You

I've been **Wanting You** for so long, my love for you is like the sweetest love song, now that I have you in my home all alone it's about to be on, I want to hold your body close to mine, is that all right? Show me a sign that it's okay if King takes you for a pleasure ride, we will be going all night, yes I been missing you and your love, your smile, your touch, baby look into my eyes you will find why I love you so much, my soul loves thee, like the sunrise you are so beautiful to me, you don't know what you mean to me, everything, you are everything I ever needed ever wanted, my dreams are forever haunted by you my love see this love will always be true, just me and you until the end of time, just you and I on this forever love making ride, can't you feel how much love I have inside, it's real the way I feel, I will marry you in a phone booth my love for you goes through the roof, this life commitment is my proof, there is nothing I want do for your love, my heart belongs to you, this is just a snippet of how I feel about you, you're loving the things that I can do when I'm pushing deep inside of your love, sitting you up while I tear it up, my love you can never get enough, wanting more of you, I have you locked in my handcuffs, my love it's about to get rough, giving you that ultimate truth as I spread your legs wide to give you my tongue surprise, lick, lick you taste just right, continuing to tongue kiss your sexy lips in between your hips, there's is not a spot I missed, I'm so in control your juices are on a natural river stream flow, coming up from being low the wetness of you dripping from my beard as I kiss your stomach saying to you I've been **Wanting You** for what it feels like a lifetime now, taking you from that lame that clown I did that, are you ready to wear a Queen's crown? This love of mine only comes around once, this is fate not luck, going deeper and deeper into the guts, feeling me in your stomach, baby my love is one hundred and eighty proof, I don't want another woman, your love is the truth I've been **Wanting You** for so long now that I have you sitting beside my throne I can call you my own, never letting go of this love, as our bodies erupts with passion, never would have thought never could have imagined you loving me, forever **Wanting You**, forever loving you and the things you do I will always stay true.

Love Power

In this shower thinking of you, your **Love Power** *has a forever hold on me, on my heart, your love is priceless like fine art, beautiful you are, making all my dreams come true, because of you I am now complete, we will get through any adversity we meet, I will go down deep as the sea if it meant you will be there waiting for me, can't you see what you mean to me, my everything under the sun with you I am someone, I feel alive, my feelings for you continue to grow deep inside, flowing through my veins since you came into my life I haven't been the same, I have no complaints when thinking of your* **Love Power***, I saw you, I called you over, you came and I conquered, we go hand and hand like a glove, I will protect you from any monster, you are my dove flying high you have my soul on fire, I don't need no water, you're my igniter, let this love burn, for you I have returned from the ashes, who would have thought who could imagine a* **Love Power** *so sweet, created just for me.*

The Big Day

Let me break this love down so you can see how this love was once found, see no matter what we went through, no matter what they said around town, no matter where in this world we were, no matter how long we been apart, I kept you close to my heart, you always stayed down, I kept our vows to never marry another unless the love compared to yours, but it's you who I adore, you are my one true love, sent from heaven's doors, my cup is filled to the top, my heart is running over with joy, full of your love, waking up to your sweet smile, oh how I love you so much, falling asleep to that sexy sound of I love you that comes out of your mouth, followed by a kiss, knocking me out, I'm ready to show you what my love is really about, morning comes around, you're up getting dress for work, not knowing what I have in store, I walk you to the door, saying I love you with a kiss and have a good day, make sure you come straight home for today will be a memorable day, you say okay I love you to my King, as I close the door and start to prepare everything, I call to make sure your ring is ready, it is, I get dressed and hop in my car thinking about how far we have come, twelve years to be exact, we have been attacked with every obstacle possible, we have had some good days and we have had some bad days, we have had some happy times and we have some sad times, but we never came untwined, with us being by each other's sides we can get through any stormy night, for your love I will *forever fight for, your heart I will never break, your heart will live in peace unharmed wrapped up in my arms, this love will continue to live on and on forever I will be soaking in your love my dove, pulling up to the place I am where I bought your beautiful ring, going inside my love I can't hide, as the teller looks me in the eyes, saying she is one lucky woman, and I replied with, no I'm a lucky man, I thank God above for putting her in my life's plan, as I spend these grands, smiling walking away saying thank you and have a nice day, on to the next phase, back in the car on my way to the florist where I order two dozen roses, one all white, meaning this is a new life, a new beginning I'm in it there will be no ending, the other set is red, a symbol of the love we have shared over the years, this teller was so nice she even gave me an extra gift for free when she found out I will be asking you to be my wife, a teddy bear with a place for a picture of me, in the shape of heart I have no doubts this love will continue to go far, paying for the stuff saying thank you as I walk to the car, on my way to the final phase the store runs, I'm stop at a red light in my sights is only you, your face can't no one compare, can't no one come in and take your place, I'm trapped in a daze called you, a horn hunks snapping me back into reality as I make that left turn and pull into park and get out moving fast, time is on my ass, grabbing a bottle of Moet and we haven't even made it to the good part yet, walking up to the counter the teller asks what's the special occasion, I say I will be* proposing to my woman today with happiness written all over my face, he says that's great you have a blessed day and good luck, I replied with a hand shake and a thanks racing home trying to get back to our place, time is flying I only have an hour until you're off and home from work, pulling up to our home, turning off my phone no interruptions, I don't have time for discussing, putting my plan to work, putting our song on repeat Just You and Me, by Raphael Saadiq, you're home not knowing what's going on, you unlock the door to come to find a mix of rose petals at your feet, trailing from the front door to the dining room table where you see there dwells a glass of Moet, and a poem written in instruction form, as you read on you continue to follow the trail of rose petals and candles up the stairs, reaching the top you begin to anticipate what I have in store for you, trying to guess what's next, and plus I haven't been found, you haven't seen nothing yet, the best is still to come as you consume another sip of your Moet before walking into our bedroom, where you see a small box and another poem covered in roses, you pick them both up and the poem states, don't open the box until you're finish reading, I love you more now than ever before, without you I can't live on, my heart is yours, my body is yours for life to explore, you I do adore, I put no one above you, you come second to none, you have my soul on fire hotter than the sun, you are my number one, you can open the box to find out what you have, watching you through a crack of the closet door, you're *surprised to find another little note saying turn around, to find me with one knee to the floor, saying you mean everything to me, I want you to forever be mine in this lifetime and the next one you are all I want under the sun, I can't live if I don't have you my one, will you do me the greatest honor of becoming my wife will you marry me? A pause- you're trying to catch your breath, tears of happiness and joy running down your face, replied with a yes, sealing it with a kiss, this is our day we will never forget, just you and me, King and Queen no jacks no spades, I will love you for the rest of my days.*

Motionless

You have my feelings; my love for you is stuck in time, stuck standing still, **Motionless**, is this real? The way you have my mind, heart, body and soul in your control my love is on hold, for my heart belongs to you, I'm giving you all of me to embrace and hold, to never let go, my heart is purer than gold, more precious than diamonds, so rare, you couldn't compare to your last, as we float off into thin air, running my fingers through your hair, nothing has ever felt so right, I'm **Motionless** until you become my wife, this jewel you will never find it, unless you look past my eyes, hiding behind my pride, you have to go deep down inside, go far for my heart, show me you will outlast the last to be in my life, everything about you is just right, if only you knew, you hold the power to freeze me in time, have me **Motionless** at any given hour your love came and conquered my soul, this love I will forever hold, I'm counting on you to come back into my life to fill my cup, to make me whole with your love, only your love can free me, I need you next to me, without your love I will forever be stuck, frozen, **Motionless** as time pass me by, waiting for that next time I can make you all mine, in this lifetime and the next, your love I can never forget.

Remember that Time

Sitting back reminiscing on the love we have share, no matter where we were, no matter who was around, no matter what time of the day or night, we didn't care, we will take each other down anywhere our love for each other showed without fear, when you gave me that look with a wink I knew it was time for me to come near, close to you, I remember every freaky little thing you used to do, **Remember that Time** *when we were driving back down to the city surrounded by the dark misty night with the stars shining real bright, mountains and trees to our left and right, you sitting in the passenger seat looking all pretty just right, you telling me you're starting to feel a little freaky can I show you my love evolved and play with your royal mic as you drive into the night, a smile comes across my face and I say I stay ready for you baby please pleasure me you can do anything you like, you begin by pulling my royal ruler out my boxer briefs, making me feel good as you kiss all over me, I need to pull over so you can feel me deep, watching out for those black and whites, opening up my door hopping out to show you what I am about, approaching your door, ready I am to explore your passionate walls, kissing you slow this love will never be revoked, as we coast I pick you up to put you on top of my hood, I'm about to make you feel real good, I slide into you with my royal wood in and out screams and shouts come from your mouth, I pull out to go south my tongue wants to show you that you* never have to doubt my pleasure I will taste you wherever, whenever, I have your palace hotter than summer's weather, nobody can do your body better, I have you howling at the moon, I'm consumed in your hot and wet womb I have you wrapped up tight as a butterfly's cocoon, right now I'm a thief, call me the palace crook the way I have your body all shook, as I come up for air it's time that I slide back in between those thighs, taking you for a never-ending forgettable ride, higher than the mountains at our side, deep into the sky your temperature rises as I push inside, flipping you over to your favorite position, that back side, I will have you busting all night long, doing your body so right, freaking and screaming, singing that love song, giving it to you nice and slowly as I go deep into your dark hole, digging you out and touching your soul, it's cold but hot as I hit your favorite spot, you say let me ride your royal cock, I want to get on top, switching position I see you on a new mission, loving this funky expedition, in this night groove digging your every move as we explode and ride off into the night's gloom, I was just sitting back **Remembering that Time** I spent being with you.

Dontae Cottrell

Familiar Love

Where did you come from? It's like you dropped high from the sky and landed in my life, but this is a **Familiar Love**, we've been here before in a different lifetime you were mine and I was yours forever to hold, our love was so strong that it came back to life in a different vessel, your touch is as soft as a rose petal, here in this new age of life, our love still holds the power, the might, we still have so much fight inside that we cannot hide, there's no top level, we keep going higher and higher, staying hotter than the devil, this love is on fire, for so long I been searching this earth for you, twenty-nine years to be exact, this is true, these are facts, your love is as serious to me as a heart attack, I need your love, I'm glad you finally made it back to me, opening my eyes wide to see, if it's you my angel, my heart, is it really you?, can I breathe, did my dreams come true, as I move in close to grab and hug you tight, looking deeply into your eyes as I slowly move towards your lips for that sweet soft kiss, that I have been missing for years, no longer alone because I have you my number one, true love that I became so familiar of, my beautiful love sent from the skies above, prayers from my lips have been answered, I've endured so much just to feel your touch once again, just to have you back in my life I missed you so much, my wife, falling back in love at first sight, shining brighter than the sun, my heart pumps for you, I am strong as a mountain my love can't be moved, I love everything you do, *from the way you smile, to the way you move, from your beautiful style to your sexy grooves, my love I am so into you, I am complete now that you're back with me, making me feel whole again, free wrapping your angel wings around me, once again I'm complete, in my past you were with me, now in the future your love still exist inside of me yet to cease, never will your love decrease, never will your love escape the warmth of my heart, my soul, I told you our love will go far, will live on even when we are gone, that's how strong our love is for one another, I can't be without you, my feelings are plain, bare not hiding undercover, thanking your father and mother for having you, I can't get enough of the things you do, my beautiful dove thanking God above for sending my one true **Familiar Love**.*

It's All about You

Tonight is not about me, tonight **It's All About You** and the things you want me to do, you're putting me in this rhythm, this groove called you, baby sit back as I undress you slowly, starting with your heels, one by one I remove as I caress and rub down your pretty feet making you feel comfortable and cozy, your smile is so sexy to me, I look deep into your eyes before pulling off your skirt feeling on your thighs as I flirt with my tongue, I'm calling you my number one, leaving your sexy thong on, you can tell by the way my royal has begun to rise I can't wait to push inside between those thighs is where I belong, forever singing your song, you are a rare diamond, the other ladies I don't mind them, moving up towards your top this room is getting hot, pulling off your shirt kissing on your neck, it's time for me to go to work, if you're scared go to church, I promise the things I'm about to do won't hurt in a bad way, but in a good way as I play with your breasts licking all over your chest, the best is yet to come, I have you steaming hot, you're second to none, taking you to a higher level, hotter than the sun and it's ninety eight degrees today, no time for child's play, you're loving the way I have your body in a twist with every kiss and every lick in between those hips, Cupid doesn't have shit on me, I'm the real love King, a beast when in between those sheets, I will have you saying encore, please repeat the things you are doing to me, I have your juices running out, making you scream and shout as you start flowing like a stream down river, you begin to quiver and shiver, clinching on my pillows, as I continue to work you low giving you that royal show, I told you, **It's All About You** tonight, just lay here and enjoy the ride as I slide in and out stroking you with all my might and power you're love I have devoured and conquered, cradling your legs, you grab my neck as I left you high to the sky, welcome to my roller coaster ride, taking your through hoops and loops, slides and dips, well-endowed and fully equipped pushing inside of your beautiful world, not holding back showing all of my acts, my moves, because tonight, **It's All About You.**

I Surrender

*My love, my heart belongs to you, it's not one thing I wouldn't do just to prove how much I'm feeling you, to you **I Surrender**, when I look into your eyes, my body and soul lose control, behold you are the one I've been searching for, your body I love to explore, from the inside out, from your intelligent mind, a woman of your stature is hard to come by, without a doubt I will forever ride at your side looking deep into your eyes as we go off into the night, I am your King and you are my Queen, see what I mean is this love will go on and on, I couldn't breathe without hearing your voice, like a R&B song I can play all day long, baby you're where you belong, grabbing you close as you scream and moan, going round and round, I love when your body is in my arms, the way I hold you close when you perform, it's nothing like the norm, I never seen these acts of love before, as we roll to the floor, I'm kissing and sucking on your bottom lip, you yearn for more, so smooth your groove is on point to, kissing you all night long I can do, what you do to me I want the world to know this love I can't hold down, can't bury it in the ground, for with me you will be wearing a Queen's crown, no more lonely nights and dealing with those non-worthy clowns, no more dark clouds, you have found a real King, a King that knows when he's finally found that one who he can't live without, no shame to have these words to be spoken out my mouth, to you **I Surrender** my love, for you are the woman the man above sent* me to love, my beautiful angel I'm so grateful I was chosen, not knowing what love was until you came along, I'm no longer frozen, you have my love groove in motion, my heart singing songs, your love so tender making me want you more and more, I'm forever yours, I can't get enough, I promise I knew you in my past life, you were my wife back in Egyptian days, and now I have returned from the grave to reclaim my place by your side, I can't resist you, the way you love me from the heart, no matter how long we have been apart, you always and will be my shining star, so to you **I still Surrender**, I need you here and near, close to me, you're my everything, not forgetting that our present is a gift, listening to you my angel as you sing I'm saying thank you to the heavens, baby all night I can watch you, talking that graveyard shift, kissing on those lips, holding those hips tightly pulling you close never letting go, each and every night it's a different act, a new show, how far will we go, I cherish every touch, every kiss with so much passion, the way you sway those hips and when I touch you dip, just does something to my love jones I can't control, I want you to have it I'm releasing the jacket, gazing upon that smile to your gorgeous brown eyes drives me wild inside, a fool for you I am, this is unconditional love, that forever love, that love that can't nobody tell me anything about your type of love, that can't nobody come in between this type of love, that satisfied love that has me flying high and above there's no coming down off your love, I just what to keep going higher and higher off your groove baby this is true, I'm a fool for you and I will do anything I have to, to prove my love, you are my dove from the skies my love **I Surrender** all of my love on bended knee right now I will marry you, my world, my kingdom, make it complete, say yes and join me on this love never-ending quest, allow my heart to come shining in your life, I want you to know right now I love you and this love is just right, my love is yours for the taking, I will give my last breath for you without hesitation, with you next to me is like my wildest dreams come true, I never knew love existed until I met you, to you **I Surrender** all that I have to offer this love will go further than any before, like a drawn out tour of the world, your world I want to forever explore, no matter what bumps and detours nothing will stand in our way, storms and lighting couldn't prevent, stop this love I have for you from getting to you, my love, as long as I have strength to say your name nothing can ever take my heart that has been given to you I know your love is true, that's why I will now and forever **Surrender** my love to you.

Under the Sun

Kissing you where the sun doesn't shine, even a blind man can find, it should be a crime the way I have your body unwinding grinding low with my tongue, I am number one, the hottest King **Under The Sun**, my love, my tongue will have you all twisted up, feeling that tingle in your gut, down your thighs and in your back it's coming on, your flow of passion raining down in record time screams of this is where I belong from you my beautiful find, as I pick you up with my arms wrapped around your spine to put you on my throne know that your body is now mine, I will own you for the night, shouts of I want to become your wife and be by your side each and every night, please you take away all my fears and frowns, I give off a charming smile continuing to show you what I'm about as I mount on top, leaving my hat on, chains and socks pushing into your special hot spot, I have your juice box on pop the way I'm knocking on your walls sliding in between those thighs, tears of joy fills your eyes, I can tell you loving the way I sway, the way I don't play when I'm rocking and moving inside, I have you feeling naughty, your soul I will ignite, your mind set on King tonight, this impression will last for the rest of your life, continuing with my pleasing, you getting weak in the knees, I have you hot, but it's cooler than a winter's breeze, you feel me deep and deep, I pull out to flip you over and spread to slide in past those cheeks, making your love talk to me, squirt, squirt, your waterfall is flowing, I have your body going berserk, call me Captain Kirk my mission is complete, as I kiss you my baby on the frontal lobe, this love I have blessed you with is more precious than anything you know, I'm blowing the competition out the water with every motion with every stroke, everlasting is the quote you will leave by my name with no complaints, can't nobody work your body out like I do going hard in the paint, there's no mistakes when I enter inside your world, your love must be fate, giving you the best groove because them other suckas can't, I'm making you howl at the moon thanking God for your lovely face, making you do what I want you to do, I knew all my feelings were right about you, I never doubted you for a second, now you're under my spell forever, **Under The Sun**, you never thought you could find a love as good as great as this one.

My Roller Coaster Ride

This will be a ride you will never forget, as I strap you in, kissing you before we begin this fantastic show, giving you a WARNING before we take off and go, **My Roller Coaster Ride** *is like no other, I'm going to swim all through your tunnel, starting off slow, cranking your body to the top as we begin to go, coasting from your feet through those thighs gazing up at those beautiful hazel eyes, your temperature begins to rise, as you continue to slide up* **My Roller Coaster Ride***, in your mind you already want to take me for another spin, put me on repeat, so we can go again, we can go all night long, this ride is built to last and it's very strong, it can handle any storm, make sure you keep your eyes open to watch me perform, finally reaching the top, we're kissing nonstop, there's no turning back, I'm about to show you my attack, my love is a different type of an act, no more clown rides, your safe, never will you replace my ride won't stop as the coaster drop, I roll low to your hot spot giving you all of what my tongue has, in and out screams of I feel you in my abs, around and around we go your hands up in the air no way can those other rides compare to* **My Roller Coaster Ride***, I told you this is a different type of ride, moving fast and swift licking towards your breasts I begin to kiss, here comes that loop to loop and tunnel as I enter inside of your gift, I have you loving what* **My Roller Coaster Ride** *can do taking you up the first loop, you're just getting a taste, a feel of what I* can really do, moving in circles as I push inside, these feelings you feeling are a surprise to you, never would you have thought I can do what I do, here comes loop number two as I go deeper inside of you, staring into those sexy eyes, yes my love I've dropped from sky, pushing your legs higher as we fly I am your knight in shining armor, not letting no harm come upon you, protecting your every little move, putting you in that ultimate groove called love, this ride my ride has taken you higher and above my love have you hooked like a drug, better than any pleasure you have had, my ride outlasts your past you're putting more scratches on my back, as I go fast and fast, smashing and dashing, your body splashing you can't hold it the ride is almost over, exploding all over the seat of **My Roller Coaster Ride** with a big smile, showing your pretty white teeth, saying thank you for the ride, I oblige with a kiss on the cheek saying you're welcome my beautiful lady, thoughts of **My Roller Coaster Ride** will stay on your mind, you're walking away remembering how I swept you off your feet until the next time we meet.

A Fool in Love

A Fool in Love is what I am, this is no game, this is not lust, but love sent from above it's hard to put into words, your love I can't get enough of, I will walk to the end of the earth to gain your trust, your love is a must have in my life, a need, a want, I never had to think twice about your hold, I crave and fiend your love, I can never let go, I'm not ashamed nor do I hide it, my dove never will I deny it, I become so excited at the very sight of you a fool for you is what I will be if it meant you will be lying next to me each and every night my heaven sent, I will fight ten men with all my might at once to prove my love is strong enough for you my heart forever burns like the sun, this is true, never will I break this bond, I can't shake your love away, say forever you will stay, **A Fool in Love**, I never can get tired or rid of your love, my Queen you are everything to me, I can't sing, but I will sing to you that's the type of fool I will be for you out in public, I wouldn't care if people tell me to shut it, with no hesitation without question this love gives me the best sensation I've ever felt, you have my feelings tossed up going round and round a mess, you make my heart melt, because of you I am not stressed, my boo, I'm loving everything you do from your sexy smile, to the way your hips move I will do anything for you, I am **A Fool in Love** not putting nobody else above, you're so special my dove never will I break this bond, this love, it's to real I can feel it deep down in my core, I can't say it enough, I could never get tired or bored of your love you are my angel from the heavens, God opened up His doors and sent you from above blessing me with your love, **A Fool in Love** is what I am, you have that can't nobody tell me nothing about your type of love, I will fly to the moon and above, oh baby I can't get enough, locking away my pride, my feelings for you are over flowing inside, there's nothing I wouldn't do for you, I will go to the top of the highest mountain to scream how much I love you, scream it loud until the whole world knows that it's you I'm talking about, your love burning deep down in my soul, a hold I can never let go, this is not a mistake, I love to wake by your side, seeing that smile so big, so beautiful and bright, lights up my life, this is a fire that can't be extinguished, baby I don't want any another woman I mean it, I'm such **A Fool in Love,** a fool for you, it's nothing I wouldn't do just to prove how much I am in love with you.

My Back Bone

You are **My Back Bone**, every King needs a spine, I am blessed that you are mine, just like fine wine this love will grow better, grow stronger with time, you will come to find there's no greater love than mine on this earth, I'm counting down the days, months and years until you give birth to my child, this love is not mild, but hot you are all I have, you take that number one spot off top you're killing the rest the way you make your body rock and pop, my love for you will never stop, will never concede you are all I need, bless the day you flew from the heavens to me, I cherish you from your head to your feet, your heart is forever with me, your beauty I will forever seek, I am forever complete, you have a hold on me that makes my soul weep, crying out for you doesn't show a sign of me being weak, it shows that you mean more to me than words, to your love I defer, you are more to me than what's under your skirt in between those thighs, I can close my eyes and see the love we share inside, I even see you when I sleep, my dreams are complete, I'm so blessed to have you in my life next to me each and every night, **My Back Bone** for life, my beautiful wife, you are more to me than what you know, this will be a forever lifetime show that will never be taken off the air, going for decades, can't nobody compare to **My Back Bone**, in your darkest hour my love will glow, illuminating your every step making sure no harm is felt, your heart I've felt beating rapidly when I come near, baby have no fear your

*King is here to protect your every move, no hurt will come to you, this is true my groove is real can't you feel my words, are you reading between the lines my girl? this love is what we both deserve, gazing into your eyes on down to those curves, I am glad you are in my world, I never have doubts about you my love, I am where I belong forever going strong, this love you can't condone, your fire keeps turning my love desire on for you, at the altar I will say I do to only you, nothing even matters anymore, without you in my life my world will feel so very small, without you baby I go through withdraws, in you I see no flaws, even the cops the law couldn't lock away my love for you, throughout our life I will continue to show you with each passing day each passing year, I will continue to prove to you why it's you I chose, why you are here **My Back Bone** I need to keep you near, my Queen, every King needs a spine, I'm so thankful your mine.*

Endless Love

This love has no time limits, it's **Endless**, never can I forget it, I couldn't live without your love inside my world you mean so much to me my girl, my woman, my Queen you are the best thing to ever happen to me, this love is so familiar to me like I've been here before, you have opened up this door to my heart, **Endless Love**, we will go far, past the stars to the end of the earth, to no point of return, from deep within I yearn for your love, I call on our heavenly father above to strengthen me with all the powers of love, I cherish you my dove, my angel from above, love is all I think of when I speak your name, when I see your frame I have no complaints when it comes to you I love everything about you, from you silky black hair to those pretty little feet, from that sexy smile to your beautiful white teeth I adore thee, you are so different so unique, I am glad it's me you chose to seek out in this world, you are so special to me, you are everything I will ever need, you fill my soul you I will never let go, you have a hold on me ever so tight, I cried the day you became my wife, my life has been complete ever since that day, that night I will cherish for eternity, for the rest of my life, for you, my heart and my soul pours out **Endless Love** that I can never get tired of.

Hold You Down

My love you are so special to me, I adore everything about you, I am here for you now and forever, no matter the weather, no matter what it is I will always **Hold You Down**, I will never change, I will always stay the same, twenty-four/seven, three hundred sixty-five, you are my piece of heaven here on earth, you set my soul on fire, I know your worth, more precious than gold your love is all I know, I'm all you will ever need, I will **Hold You Down** through every altercation I put no one above you, (muah) blowing a kiss just for you, I love you and only you, my heart is yours this is a fact, I belong to you, this is no act, I'm your forever knight in shining armor, no drama, no harm will come to thee, allow me to sweep you off your feet, no storm, no rain can keep you away from me, I will forgive any mistake can't you see with me your love is here to stay, I will continue to mend your broken heart and take away your pain, this love is easy to explain, because it's true, it's real not fiction or fake, my heart smiles when I'm awake to see you by my side, this love is no lie I will give my life for you to live on knowing our love will live on when I'm gone, yes my love is that strong, my soul performs a love song when in your arms, I'm at home close the door, you will never be alone again I spin and spin around the question, how did you come into my life and take my heart, you keep me guessing, by far have given me more pleasure with just gracing me with your presence than anyone before sent from heaven's doors, from deep within my core, my love, my heart pours out in love for you, it's an honor to be next to you, **Holding You Down**, keeping you away from the fools and clowns, I'm a King and you're the jewel in my crown my Queen taking away your frowns, I take it personal if I see a tear drop to the ground from your face, I'm here to erase those bad memories and introduce you to this love sympathy, when it comes to you nobody can tell me anything you mean everything to me can't you see, I will do the utmost to please thee, to please you I will do whatever you ask of me whatever it takes to see that smile upon your beautiful face, for the rest of my life I will be your King and love you, with the blessing from above our love will fly high, there's no limit we can't reach, baby believe me you are not dreaming when we are between those sheets, I can teach you a groove that will make your body forever move, this love, my love will make you preach to the public letting the people know you don't put nobody else above it, above me, telling the next man there's no need to compete, King is the best thing to ever happen to me, my eyes are clear, I can see you are all I need, it's easy to be here for you, **Hold You Down** in everything you do, I have so much love for you this is true, I will forever be here to **Hold You Down**, we are forever me and you.

My Rib

*Let me break it down so this love will forever be clear to you, you were made from **My Rib**, your love will forever flow through my body and soul, never will I revoke the power of your love, you are a special gift made for me, from me, by the man above, you are everything I need, my heart pumps and bleeds your love, our life, our love is blessed by the heavens above, under the sun we are one, you were made to share nothing, but beautiful, passionate and caring love with me, there's no limit we cannot reach together, my heart will forever live inside you, apart we will never be, through your eyes I see we will get through any test we can handle any mission, through your eyes I see that you will honor, respect and hold me up when I'm down not at my best, there will be no remission from you I see it through your eyes, I feel what you feel this love will never rest, but only rise higher and higher beyond the sky, through my eyes **My Rib** you will continue to be here for me when I am in need and stand at my side when I am weak, these are some of the things I see when I look at you my lady, you even make sure to pray for me, we are connected spiritually, your love forever I will seek you are here to complete me, I am nothing without thee, without you my heart will never move, will never pump, will never feel that special groove, I will be stuck in time until you came back into my life to comfort me, make me whole and put me back in that love mood, being with you puts a smile on my* soul, you were made from **My Rib** to teach me how love goes, encouraging my every-day goals staying close and never letting go, you have a hold so firm so tight, reminding me that I am not alone you will walk with me and set beside my throne for the rest of our lives, I don't have to worry about any hurt or harm, you shine so brightly through the night, your love performance is just so right, for this love I will fight for with all that I have, that look you give me sends my feelings on blast, out of this world, chills down my spine your love is outta sight, you're all mine holding your love tight with all my might, yes you were made from **My Rib** for me, to be by my side for all time, this love can't be torn apart it is too divine, this love was already written in our book of lives, you were made from **My Rib** so that we can spend life together, I will forever cherish the ground you walk on, my love performance is strong, with you bearing my children and raising them right I know that my legacy will live on, **My Rib** your heart will always live inside of mine for all time I know I could never find another like you., you were made for me, but I want nothing else, but to please you, in my eyes you are all I know all I see, I will love thee until I am deceased.

My Gift

Today is the day that I give you something special, something dear to me, a gift that has never been given away before, you have come into my life and made me explore this feeling called love, as I stand here before you bearing your gift, know that you are **My Gift** sent from above, moving on and on my feelings for you are racing up as you lick your lips, I must say it's nothing visible, but it's something you have been wanting so long for, something that you want so much to call your own, know that this is love not a crush or lust, you touch me in so many different ways, you're standing here wondering what it is I'm trying to say, trying to figure out this special gift I have for you today, asking questions, you are trying to gather hints, I'm letting you know without hesitation I'm willing and ready to take a risk, this love I will never quit I must admit you have my body, heart, mind and soul in a twist, looking in your eyes I see the reaction I'm about to get, so I hit you with it as you blow me a kiss filled with love, you are so special to me my beautiful dove, **My Gift** to you is my heart, I am with you now and forever we will never part, we will go far on this journey of love nothing will stand in our way I hold the power of love, never have I spoken these words and now I'm ready happy to say, I love you and it's nothing more I want than to be with you for the rest of my days, keeping you in my world for the rest of your life, is that fine with you, is that alright? Tears dropping from your eyes to my surprise you hop in my arms with a soft whisper of I love you and yes I will be with you for the rest of our lives, the sky now shines so brightly we're holding each other tightly, our faces pull back just enough to look into each other's eyes falling into a trance, your spell has me overwhelmed, our smiles so big and wide, while my heart melts inside I never thought this day would ever enter my life, reaching with my lips to embrace you with a kiss filling my soul, you have a hold on me that I can never let go, this is so you are my forever we belong together, dancing to our own music, creating a rhythm without a song, for the rest of our lives this beat will play on and on, never will you ever be alone, our hearts are united as one, I bless the day you drop from the sun, reaching an ultimate climax without any sexual content, this is how I knew our love was meant, together forever my love will never bend or break, your love I can never shake, hold **My Gift** for the rest of your days.

My Love Planet

It's time I came to your world and take you to another level, from **My Love Planet** *I've been watching you and I see you have been dealing with these dudes who are not worthy enough to be with you, I see they haven't given your body what it needs, when you are with me I will make sure you're the one who's pleased, take my hand and allow me to ease your mind, body and soul, do you think you're ready to explore* **My Love Planet**? *I will be sure to complete you and make you whole, I hope you can handle and manage what I'm about to do to you, my love will never fold, you will never want to let go, so prepare yourself we are about to take flight and go to a new world, my world, letting you know my sex intelligence makes every other man irrelevant, no need to be nervous or scared my love when you step into my spaceship, baby beware I'm fully equipped with all the right tools, I can't wait to get inside of you and show you all my moves and grooves, we will be going through the stars past the moon to my galaxy, I am your fantasy come true, don't worry you will be safe with me I have you, I begin to count down the seconds until we lift, five, four, three, two, one, kissing your lips lights me on fire and has me hotter than the sun, warmer than the summertime, your lips are so soft, your kisses are so divine, we blasting off to* **My Love Planet** *we will be there in no time, I am in control, we're in the middle of darkness where there's no road, my love just relax your mind, body and let go, just* *float as I coast through your curves my heart feels an electric surge, as I enter your black hole tickling your soul making your body glow with the color passion of love, we're so high up you out shining the stars below they should come above and ask if they can shine and glow with some of your love, you're loving the way I have you in motion on float, here comes that juicy white flow as I start to stroke and stroke that back side, we looking down watching over earth making space our paradise, you're scratching and moaning whispers of you wanting to be love by me for life, I'm not finished yet making you blast off twice, we will be going all night, going for hours, no I won't stop until you rain down like a meteor shower,* **My Love Planet** *has the power to conquer and devour anything in its path you feel my might, my wrath with every touch, every stroke of my milky way, words you cannot speak, you cannot say, your expression on your face says it all, as my giant rocket keeps flying through those walls hitting that spot, hitting that pocket, no I can't stop it baby don't fight it, let it go, you've never seen, you've never felt a show like mine, the way I have your body unwinding you're finding it hard to resist, there's no tapping out I won't let you quit until I hit you with this, flipping you around face to face grabbing you at your waist pulling your torso close, wrapping your legs around me low as I slide in lifting you high it's time for my rodeo ride, taking it slow as I go and go you never had it like this before, after this we will stick a flag on the moon, the first couple to ever make love on planet*

Neptune, as I zoom and zoom through the halls of your palace, did you ever imagine this love, us fitting like a glove, tight, my rocket is full of fuel, going longer than the night can last, I'm ready to blast off inside of you, legs of mine are getting weak, I'm reaching my peak letting it go, giving you all of me, making sure I leave you with an lasting impression out in my galaxy, from **My Love Planet**, back to your planet earth I showed you my world, my worth, my girl anytime you think of me, just look up in the skies and remember this never forgetting night and close your eyes and call my name and I will be right at your side ready to give you more of the same, my love is extraordinary, never plain and ordinary, this experience you had on **My Love Planet** can't be buried.

My Girl Bad

Where do I start, the love we share is priceless art, our love shines brighter than any star, no matter where you are I will travel far, oh you bad, you so bad, I've always known what I had, but damn when I'm thinking of you alone I can picture you all up on it, all up on me, kissing me in all the right places, riding me until the morning rise, smiling faces, oh you so bad looking like a bag of money, before you that was the only thing I wanted, my heart smiling means you have me caught up in this moment, **My Girl Bad**, you're the only thing I'm wanting, I'm so glad it's me you chose to unclothe, head first when I dive into your palace of love, lick, lick when I touch, praising you up, while I take you down, no this is not lust, as I begin to cut and cut away, soft not rough, my loving is official, so good to where you can't get enough, me staying temporary never, this love will last forever, this King is very clever when playing on your playground, I will have your mind going round and round the way King put it down, wiping away every frown I'm no clown when inside your town, laying your body down in different positions, can you handle this mission, no more fishing I found what I've been missing, making you rain, yea you dishing out that waterfall, as I slide in between them halls, screams and shouts from the neighbors coming through the walls, I'm a shark down there call me Jaws, going deep into your warm dark hole, that feeling has come for you to let go, my stroke is so official, breaking you down, but lifting you up we're dripping sweat like we're out playing in the sun, **My Girl Bad** so bad I can't help, but call her number one, I love everything you do with your tongue you are the one for me to be with for the rest of my life this love passion I will not lose, as we keep going off into the night, blessed I am to have you in my life, you complete King, you are my Queen and not just because you wear the crown, it's because you hold down everything that words means to me, which is being my lover, my best friend and being the perfect mother for my children, you are one in a million the way you hold down my throne when I am gone away from home, our love making is just a plus, you mean so much more to me than just a nut, I told you this was not lust, but love, I meant what I said until I am dead I will love you and even then in your dreams I will come to you, for without you I am not complete, my soul will never be able to sleep until you are lying next to me, **My Girl Bad**, so bad, I wouldn't be who I am today, if I never had what I have, this I can say I will love you each day in different ways.

Promise Land

My lady come and take my hand, let me lead you to my **Promise Land**, where you won't be able to withstand my love passion, your feelings will blast off once I lay you across my bed starting low going in between your legs while you rub on my head open up so I can be fed, no need to be scared I stay prepared there's no need to go anywhere flying high in the air we will, where your feelings will be revealed as I kill all your doubts and fears, this love I possess will live on inside of you for years and years to come as a single tear rolls from your eye down the side of your right cheek, my love comes at a price and it's not cheap, as I continue to pleasure you and make you weak, you fucking up my sheets your wetness is all over me, you shouting out you getting the best of me, I'm loving everything about your physic your body will be the death of me, I can't see nothing, but you next to me, right by my side living in my arms for the rest of your natural lives, my **Promise Land** is nothing like the norm, especially when I lift you up to give you that royal attack your legs wrapped around my back as I begin to perform, all night I will keep going and going consuming your love your head rolls back as your eyes shoots to the stars above, your my number one my favorite melody the sound of you take me high so heavenly, the way you're blessing me as you continue to sing out, turning into a chef, I'm your cook baby I have that recipe you need stroke after stroke making you believe can't nobody do your body like me, sexing you down, multiple stimulation is what you have found, you're loving the way I bring your waterfall down, I have you going crazy, going wild to no surprise I keep making your passion rise and rise setting a fire ablaze through your body straight to your soul this love I have for you I can't control, you have a hold on me that can never be broken my passion grows for you with every kiss with every stroke and every touch keeping me afloat on cloud nine you're doing the most to my feelings this love you could never find, I am a rare breed one of a kind going higher than cloud nine on ten with me in your life you can't lose, you will do nothing, but win, baby let's get married so we're not living in sin you are who I want until the end, so say yes you will take my hand and forever be in King's land, my royal plan is solid guaranteed indeed my love will fulfill your every need, my love belongs where your heart pumps and bleed, imbedded deep inside you, this is the honest truth I will never stop loving you.

Memoirs of a Royal Lover

The First Time

It is nothing like **The first Time**, I'm trying to tell you I can blow your mind, with just a simple touch of my lips to your soft skin you will feel the power I hold within, let's begin as I run my hand down your spine looking deep into your eyes a single kiss brings your love passion to a rise, running my fingers through your hair turning you around so you can stare through the mirror as I start to kiss with a soft lick to the back of your neck raising your arms to pull off your shirt I flirt and flirt with my hands on your sexy breasts we just started and your palace is soaked and wet, you haven't seen nothing yet turning you back face to face picking you up and setting you on the counter, so that my tongue can encounter what's below your waist between your thighs, I can tell from the look in your eyes that you never felt a tongue like mine, going deeper in between those thighs you're getting weaker screams from you that you're a keeper, making you warmer than the summer time I raise up from being down in between your palace for quite sometime, it's nothing like your lips and the way our tongues roll and twist, tasting like a red Jolly Rancher candy, I hope you're ready to become my miss, picking you up to lay you on my California King, as I become undressed pulling out that royal stick, I know this is our first time, but the way you rose up grabbed and licked, you would think we've been here before making me scream out oh my lord the way you're performing with your tongue, *has me thinking you are the one I been looking for, I'm so ready to explore this passion all night everlasting, satisfaction indeed as I lay you back to give you what you need, starting off slowly letting you feel each and every stroke, deeper and deeper I go giving you an outstanding show as we float and float on high, gazing into your beautiful eyes pulling your thighs towards my chest as I give you the best you ever had, moving a little faster this will be an happily ever after pushing all the right buttons, I have your body hotter than Chef Ramsey's oven, wet like a lake as I push inside of your walls staying hard never going soft you telling me pull out you want to stroke me with your mouth, I lay on my back telling you to sit on my face sixty-nine style let me taste you again for a while, curled toes and bodies yearning giving each other that good, good loving, you stroking my royal wood as I am licking you oh so good, turning that ass around so you can hop on top, you begin riding me like you running from the cops making that nice apple bottom pop as your legs begin to lock you cumin' all over my royal cock you continue nonstop I sit up to kiss your lips on to your neck down your breasts showing you I'm better than the rest, wrapping your legs around my waist before I stand to give you a taste of my strength going deeper within touching your soul this love you will never want to let go as I stand stroking you slowly showing you how far I can go pressing you up against the wall making you wetter than a waterfall giving you all nine inches and this is just the beginning, I* have your head spinning and spinning with me your winning, a hour strong into it, (pause) as I pull out of your walls to set you down and turn you around, dropping to my knees to spread your cheeks look at this lips dripping wet smiling at me, kissing and licking in between making you weak as I please you're cumin' all over me, I stand to land my flying rocket into your wet palace, you yelling out oh my god don't stop it I'm cumin' again going deeper from the back giving you that King attack pulling on your hair as I arch your back, smack, smack, smack is the sound the neighbors hear, leaning forward to kiss you, lick you soft on the ear, with me there's nothing to fear the end is near I feel it in my legs calves getting tight I begin to stroke with all my might faster and harder, faster, faster you are all that matters, screaming out I'm about to cum baby you are the one thing I want under the sun, blasting off busting like a desert eagle to you there's no equal as our bodies unwind just think this was our **First Time**.

My Love Slave

Tonight, you are **My Love Slave**, all week you have misbehaved, grabbing you by the hand leading you down to my love cave, I can see in your eyes you can't wait, which makes me believe you have been misbehaving on purpose, knowing that the punishment will be worth it, walking you down the stairs where there lies my bed, a chair no windows so the neighbors can't hear, yes you should fear for what I'm about to have you do, lights come on my camera is pointed to watch you perform, before I sit in my chair, I tell you to strip down you smile, tonight is about to get wild as I walk towards my closet to grab my erotic pleasures, this love can't be measured, handcuffs and chains you've been a bad girl tonight I'm not playing, I turn around to find you naked seconds pass I walk over to you pulling you close grabbing you by your ass kissing your lips pushing you away as I flip the script, telling you to tie your hair up in a ponytail so I can see all of you when you begin to go low and give me that mouth, lip, tongue action show, I sit in my chair grabbing my remote to turn on something slow, putting you in the groove you begin to dance and move, nice and sexy you take a few shots of the Remy it's about to get hectic, putting you in the mood I can see your body is ready, I take a few myself as you do what you do thrusting your hips, swaying your way towards me as you turn and twist, my eyes have become engaged, you're giving a show I couldn't miss, the heat has risen in this cave, you turn around and dip popping that ass making my eyes do flips coming up slow licking your lips, I take another sip knowing I'm about to embark on a never-ending trip, I tell you to give me a lap dance you slide over placing your hands on my legs feeling the bulge in my pants as you grind bending over showing me your sexy dance I can see your palace dripping wet and I haven't even touched you yet, but you can bet you will be dripping more than ever before once I begin to touch and play with your insides, I hope you can endure, I unbuckle my pants and tell you to take your hands and pull out my royal snake and begin to lick and lick until he's fully awake before he takes his natural place into your walls, for now your mouth and jaws will do work as you start in showing me what a bad girl you've been, hard as a rock I am loving the way you deep throating giving me that royal Queen top, stroking with both hands and mouth as your tongue give off that soft wetness showing me why you're the best putting all my doubts to rest, you come up with a lick to my chest a lick to my neck a passionate kiss to my lips, backing away as you sway and dip to Usher's Trading Places, I give you a signal to move back my way, you come with your back towards my front, a kiss to your cheek as I whisper and say I hope you ready for me, my right hand begins to slide up the inside of your thighs, playing with your pearl tongue as I stand and rise kissing you up your back towards your shoulders, Casanova don't have shit on me he might as well move over the way I'm about to *please your soul I have a hold on you that you can never break loose from or let go, pushing you to the floor your body I begin to explore my hands have a mind of their own once they get going I can't stop them, you look so good on film, starting off with a massage from your head to your toes, touching you where the sun can never go, kissing you from your toes to your head I'm ready to be fed, sucking on your lovely breasts your nipples hard as I caress, licking down your hourglass at last I'm where I'm supposed to be, glad I am, but I stop and pause telling you to get up off the floor lay on my bed so I can spread you wide before I tongue you down, crawling into my bed, you are the sexiest thing I've seen so far in my time the essence of fine, but not getting off track laying on top of you kissing you soft as I grab your hands locking them together putting the handcuffs on both securing you to the bed post, moving down towards your hips and thighs sliding off the bed taking your right leg to tie up with my chains that smile on your face I can tell you're liking this little game we're playing, turning you on even more I'm so ready to explore, but not before I take your left leg chaining you to the bed, now that your spread wide open I want you to close your eyes and focus, going to my closet of erotic pleasures again to grab that hot baby oil, making your skin softer as I begin rubbing your body down you feel my tongue going round and round on every part of your body, your palace can't fight it as I play with your pearl making your girl explode that's what I was looking for, as I go down* south to give you more licking as I thrust with two fingers your temperature's rising your body so excited as I lick deep inside your walls you've been going throw withdraws, that's why you been acting out in all, you whisper King put your royal snake inside of me I want to feel you deep, I come up with that wet sticky face no time to waste I guide my royal to that special place giving you a taste going slow stroke after stroke you want to grab me close, but you can't tonight you're **My Love Slave** and in this cave I am King giving you that royal thing all you can do is scream and shout, singing you are the greatest coming out your mouth as I show you what I am about picking up the flow as I go and go faster and harder your legs spread so far apart I'm going deeper by far past the stars into a different element this passion is the business, this action was meant to be I am feeling weak, I'm at my peak your palace will be the death of me, you saying give it all to me please explode your seeds inside of me make me complete, looking into each other's eyes as I let go inside kissing you slow letting you know I love you and only you **My Love Slave** I can never let go.

Dontae Cottrell

A Feeling You Never Felt Before

I'm asking you right now at this very moment are you ready for what I can give you what I will offer you? To be honest your heart deserves more than what the normal man can give you, I love everything about you and willing to show you, just sit back and listen to what I have to say and at the end you can tell me if we can do the unthinkable, baby believe me I'm all that you will ever need, I am the end of your search you prayed enough in church, your true love stands right before you, I will do the utmost to show you what it means to be loved, our love my love can't be ignored, baby are you ready to explore life with just me, can't you see, can't you feel what I feel deep inside this love for you is ready to burst explode from the inside out without a doubt I'm ready to clip my wings why because I won't be flying away like the rest, you are imprinted within my chest you are my angel sent to relieve my stress, the best thing my soul has found and you can bet, I want nothing more than to marry you do this thing right, close your eyes my love look beyond the clouds can you see us in your sights, I will be there to wipe away any tears there will be no fear because I will forever be here, forever be nearby your side, see my love I don't want half of you I will be only cheating myself, I want the whole package I can just imagine us growing old together being strong for one another, fighting to get through any stormy weather, I will do anything to show you there is no one else better than me, my love I don't have much, but I'm willing to give all my possessions up for your love willing to try anything to keep you by my side never will I stop loving you, everything about you puts a smile on my heart and did I mention our love making part, yea that part is just a plus each and every day it will be a must no it's not lust, but love, my love with you I can accomplish anything in life go far and beyond, swim through any sea, lake, river or pond, will fly beyond to the stars and moon just to be with you, there's nothing no one can say to me about you that can ever change my heart, my mind I want you for all time for the rest of my life, open your eyes baby to find me on bended knee kissing you at your feet giving you all of me I will, I am here to please you and only you, so tell me with this ring in my hands what do you want you to do? Please say yes, say you want me to for the rest of your life, before my love can answer.... (Pause)...a light knock on my door I wonder who can that be... (To be continued...).

Rain Drops

It's midnight and I can't sleep wishing my love, my world was next to me so that I can tease and please her body and soul, forget this where is my phone, dialing my baby's number waking her out of her slumber, still sounding so sexy to me, hey baby it's me are you sleep, she replies with a yes, but I'm up now what's wrong, oh nothing baby I just wish I can be next to you I need you and want you bad in the worse way If I must say, I want to taste your body, I want to kiss your face, I want to taste your breasts and lick below your waist, that is just some of my many wishes on this stormy night can I come over and please your body, mind and soul, you have this hold on me I need to be inside thee so I can sleep, plus you know how the rain makes me feel, my freaky side becomes unveiled, your taste is my desire, so delicious, it's kind hard to fight it once my fire is ignited, can you feel my heart beat babe through the phone you have me so excited, she answers with a yes my King, but please be careful its pouring down raining hard and you're driving from afar, you mean so much to me, you are my everything, I say ok will do will text you when I'm close, tonight we will be making love faces baby I love you see you soon, let's not waste another second, hitting my end button tossing my covers and hopping out of bed to the bathroom my feet led/split screen on the other side my love is up washing her face and in between sipping on some wine with the phone nearby waiting for her King to arrive sitting in her thong with nothing, but her robe on, on my side walking through my garage hitting my alarm to my Porsche sparking my cigar as I smoke, smoke, smoke thinking about the different positions I'm going to have my love in when I stroke, stroke, stroke, keys in the ignition car in reverse hitting the gas here I go, it's pouring down hard as fuck and they say it never rains in California, but nothing will stop me from getting up on her, my love we go hand and hand like a baseball glove to a bat once I pull into her driveway I'm going to show her my King attack, but let's stay focus because it's pouring, I barely can see I don't want this night to be the death of me, twenty minutes have passed and I can do nothing, but think about how soft my baby's ass will feel when I touch and grab, squeezing soft pulling you close another twenty miles to go I'm doing eighty, but it feels like I'm driving slowly just a few other cars are on float, but can't keep up with my flow, I'm on a mission a funky expedition, a text comes through it's my baby boom, hey where are you? I'm worried, are you close babe, I replied, getting off on your exit now at the light I'm about to come around the corner get ready for a long night, as I pull up in my lady's drive way I see her standing in the doorway ready for her King, drink in her hand and a cigar spark just for me, she is all I need, I can't explain the feeling it's an amazing thing she's like a prize possession, a gift to a King, putting my car in park I see she put her drink down and left my cigar at the door as she walks over I get out my car closing the door no words were spoken pulling each other close feeling this love potion, it's raining hard on top of our heads, but I'm ready to be fed not wasting no time my love is so fine pulling off my shirt looking into her eyes I can see she's loving the way the rain is running down my chest this is about to be the best night yet, as I rub up her thighs kissing her lips like never before picking my love up putting her on my hood so I can go down and become full with her ecstasy, baby just watch and see you haven't seen nothing yet giving you all of me, the greatest love you ever felt never have you dealt with a King like me, there is none like me as I lick and suck on those lips below this rain isn't stopping my King show, it's not the rain, but me sending chills down your spine, putting you on float, you say I want to taste and deep throat standing up pulling down my sweats giving me the best, all hands on deck, I whisper I want to be inside of thee, you stand I kiss you, turn you around grabbing you at the waist you putting that arch in you back as I slide in slow making sure you feel my royal, every inch of me I'm so deep you feel me in your stomach already you cumin' all over my royal pipe this may last all night the way I feel, this feeling I feel for you is too real beyond my wildest dream you are everything I will ever need whispering those words soft in your ear baby I want to forever be here inside of your love I am your eagle and you are my dove, stroke after stroke screams of baby go deep as you can go taking my hands spreading you wider so I can go deeper inside her, inside your palace, this royal is only for you and only you and you replied as is she, my palace is all yours and only yours for you to do what you want and explore to the fullest the sky is not the limit of where we can go, pulling my royal out turning you around I want to see your face kissing you softly your lips fills my heart, as I raise one leg to slide back in I begin to dance all up in your palace showing you I can work my hips like magic, round and round up and down I'm your fool only a clown for you placing your legs above you as I continue to please you through the **Rain Drops** coming down in slow motion as I rock your body from coast to coast, I have you at my mercy as you feel me deep within your comfort zone I will never leave you alone as you moan and moan those sweet sounds as I'm about to cum again baby, pound, pound as my legs weaken mine is coming around as I dwell inside your palace, every time it rains your love is all I will be able to think of and imagine, my **Rain Drops**.

She Isn't You

After I lost you my true love, I have come into contact with what you call a distorted vision, seeking women of your stature it's like I'm a slave and your my master, even though you're gone out my life my heart is at a standstill, I don't carry that will to love another the way I loved you when you were by my side, I'm hoping one day you will come back and be my wife, see what I mean every women I allow in my life I measure them to you, the feeling the love never lasts because **She Isn't You**, *It's the little things that you used to do that have me missing you, like your laugh your smile the way you go wild screaming out all those freaky sounds when I used to touch there and there yes everywhere, the gaze we gave off looking into each other's eyes, your lips our kiss ever so soft feeling my heart with love I hate I gave you up, baby come back and fill my cup with your love we can share the world go up and above I still care about you and your love, the way we used to fit like a glove, the way you used turn me on, the way you used to have me hot yearning for your sweet love, I forever think this passion will live on and on, am I wrong for thinking about you when another is in my arms, wishing it was you I was kissing, touching and licking, sticking and moving inside of your palace closing my eyes just to imagine it's you on top of me, giving me everything I need, I'm starting to think it's something wrong with me, sometimes I can't even sleep, having to make up lies for reasons why I* stay up at night to the one lying next to me, I've tried to move on and break loose of this bond, your hold, but with this other woman I feel cold and alone, she can't ignite my fire my passion my love the way you can, **She Isn't You** can never do the things you can do, I even complain about how she cooks her food nothing is never too good and maybe it's just me, but I can't let it be I can't allow her to get to close forever my heart is closed until I know our love is ghost, I'll keep our memories close in mind I feel like I'm in jail doing time lost in the desert somewhere waiting for you to come near, I will do anything to be back with you, it may be wrong, but I will drop the one I'm with because **She Isn't You** and can't do the things you can do, I don't know what it is you have done to me, but it has me acting in ways I can't explain, there have been times I called your name when inside of another dame, why is this happening to me, is it your loving that has my door open I can't believe this one bit I never thought this could happen to me a King she was the one who was supposed to wear my crown, my ring, I miss everything about you, woman after woman who came after you just can't meet my qualities and do me the way you used to, because **She Isn't You** my one true love the one I can never let go of.

When Your Love Calls

In the late night hour my phone rings, it's you my freaky Queen, asking did I wake you are you busy or anything, I hope this isn't a bad time, but you are running circles through my mind, a slight laugh comes out on my end replying with no it's ok your call will be accepted at any time of the day or night, I can be anywhere when you call on me and I will be there, dropping whatever I am doing just to get to you, to fulfill your dreams, your fantasy and your needs, with a smile on your face you say well in that case I need you to come and make my dreams, my fantasy, and my needs my reality, I'm in need of some sexual healing your love is what I want to be feeling right now how does that sound, I reply it sounds like tonight is about to be wild, unlock your door and just wait patiently for me to come into your room and climb in between your sheets pour me a drink light a few candles and be naked for me, you say ok we hang up with I'll see you in a minute I'm on my way, hopping in my ride listening to French kiss thinking about how good you will feel when I'm inside hitting it until you tap and quit, I arrive opening the door I hear soft music playing coming from inside your room I enter with a smile it's time to lay down the boom, words fall from my lips as I grab my glass and take a sip, my love I've been waiting for your call you're the only one I've been able to think of, just lay there because tonight it's all about you it's not about me I am your freak, we don't need any covers just those silk sheets I can't wait for those thighs and legs to be wrapped around me, enough talking I set my glass down and began to walking what I preach, giving you a little strip tease, making you wet in between those knees you open up playing with the inside of your thighs, the temperature in this room is at a rise, keeping your eyes focus on me, are you ready for me to fulfill your needs, can I make you weak, taking it up a notch I have the key to open up your Pandora box, your last didn't do it right if you haven't had it quite like this, let me flip the script as I dip to the kitchen to grab some chocolate syrup and some strawberries after tonight you will want to marry me, I'm doing something new, baby tonight it's about you it's not about me as I feed you these chocolate covered strawberries blowing your mind you will never find another of my kind as I unwind your body you getting so excited as I take it to the next level pouring chocolate all over your pleasure points my loving is on point, I have you blazing smoking like a joint, anointing your body igniting your fire as I lick in between and inside your thighs giving it to you just right with my tongue making your heart skip beats the way I'm freaking, you're breathing harder biting the sheets your dripping like water your body is calling as I swim through your walls, no more stalling just let it flow baby let go and explode your love, you taste like candy I'm in heaven and your my dove flying high as I take you higher than before my tongue has done enough exploring it's time to get hardcore just relax no need to be on the defense while I'm on the attack, there's pleasure in this pain I'm about to drive your love insane, for now I am fully naked are you ready for this second pleasure no need to measure you will feel me deep in your stomach just looking at him you feel yourself cumin', spreading you wide kissing you soft before I push inside, strap in baby and hold on tight for this will be a bumpy ride for the rest of the night, taking my time stroking you slow, giving your body what it deserves and more as I go deeper exploring your every twist and turn making you yearn screaming loud, pillow to your face as I tell you to wrap your legs around my waist showing you my strength, standing tall with ease you dropping the pillow to the floor your arms surround my neck as I grip your cheeks, giving you this pleasure and pain show, sending chills up your spine, there's no thrill like this thrill, no love making like mine, taking my time with each stroke after stroke making you cum more and more that was number three and I'm not close to being weak as I bend at the knees to lay you back down I see no frowns, but all smiles as I pound and pound picking up the pace as I swim through you place, your treasure no matter the weather I will come **When Your Love Calls**, just to be in between your walls sweating you out, to hear you scream and shout trading affection, going for hours my beautiful flower as I devour you hole whipping you back and forth turning you around so I can give you the most, first we going to coast as I rock your boat going slow so that you can feel every inch of me in every stroke loving the way your body feels next to mine, you belong to me your body is forever mine and I place no one above you, sliding your hair to the side so I can kiss your back side, the mirror is in plain sight, we're looking just right as I push deeper inside you moan and sigh with pleasure making you feel real good like a real King should, giving you those X's and O's, when it comes to me I always give a royal show, putting that arch deep in your back taking you up as I put it down you so fly as I hit you from behind harder and harder, making your squirt meaning you're flirting with cumin' again for the fourth time at the right time, keeping that arch in your back as mine begins to arrive, I tell you to hold it for a few more minutes stay on track at the heart we will always be attached, you finally met your match, we both climax at the same damn time, we will be trading places, next time you will find yourself in my room giving me all of you, **When My Love Calls**... (To be continued).

Exploring Your Body

*Thoughts running through my head of you, of the night I came over to do the things you wanted me to, I remember how I walked through your door willing and ready to explore each and every part of your body, just thoughts of you is getting me so excited all over again, not wanting that night to ever end so I took my time, kissing you from head to toes holding your body ever so close, no thoughts of ever letting go cross my mind my beautiful find loving the way you wind and glide that body of yours as I explore deep down to your core, giving you more and more, touching you softly lights off candles burning we've moving to the rhythm of the music yarning with passion, your love I could never lose it, I couldn't even image, **Exploring Your Body** from your neck to your chest you haven't seen nothing yet I am the best at what I do I can't wait to be inside of you, to show you my moves the way I groove when pushing in and out without a doubt I can take you higher, suspended in the air, having you scream the words sire, my love I came prepared as I take you there our hearts are one I haven't touched you there yet, but you yelling you're about to cum, I have you hotter than a summer's day, I'm not here to play any games I know you have dealt with those lames before me, you never dealt with a real King, but I am here now look at what you have found a real man who have you falling sinking deeper than quicksand, as I begin **Exploring Your Body** my tongue enters your land* your thighs rise high above my head, your hands rubbing up and down my back licking you softly, kissing your lips even softer playing with your pearl tongue I am your number one, the things I can do can never be repeated or done I am the only one who can have your body rocking there's no stopping your body is popping your speechless as I take my time to give you what you need my mission is to succeed and I won't stop until I do, making you explode again with me you can't do nothing, but win, as I begin to take you to another level, I'm about to have you hotter than the devil, **Exploring Your Body** putting my royal shaft inside where only darkness can hide, taking my time exploring each curve giving you what you deserve with each stroke, I begin to coast through your walls, my love is so powerful you're running like the law is after you with the way I'm pushing inside of you, sweating it out with no words falling from your mouth, your expression says it all, grinding slow making you lose your mind, baking your body like a cake freaking you from the night until the day, my legs begin to shake, **Exploring Your Body** is the best thing that could ever have happened to me I must say.

Unforgettable Night

This will be an **Unforgettable Night**, my love my passion holds the might, the strength of ten men, can't nobody do it better than I can, baby take my hand let me lead you to my lover's land, I have a master plan, just allow me to do what I do and let my tongue land where it needs to land, up and down your spine tonight your all mine not taking my time, I have no time to waste stripping you down picking you up laying you on the bed to lick below your waist, I love the way your passion tastes, you have me coming up with that sticky face, I have you on the run and yes I am on the chase, judging by your sounds you want it and you need it right now, I'm here to put something special in your life, giving it to right, I love to go hard you can't measure how high I'm going to raise the bar, as I take you there by far the best you ever had you can't compare as I kiss you there and there and in your special place once again I'm loving the way you taste, so sexy and sweet to me, you're about to bring the freak up out of me, reaching deeper into you with my fingers, the sounds coming from you are lingering down the halls as your love falls, I'm raising up to kiss you from your breasts to your lips from your lips to licking you on your ear down to your neck and back again to those nice voluptuous breasts of yours, tonight I'm part of Dora's crew as I explore your sexy body, it's all about you, baby grab my neck and watch what I'm about to do, give you all of me as I grip your legs with my arms ready to give you a performance you've never seen or felt before, my feet is the only thing touching the floor as I rock your body back and forth, giving you that French kiss sucking on your bottom lip making your body drip, X's and O's expressing my affections, I promise you will never get it like this putting you down turning you around spreading your cheeks to give you all of me, I have your body weak as you bust all over me, jumping off in your body taking off, lifting off making sure you feel me taking you deep, pulling you closer to me, kissing on your shoulders there's no other better lover under covers, murdering your insides giving it to just right my love is outta sight, you should write a book on how I lay my pipe, pushing with all my might grabbing your hair as I take flight, taking you there, this I swear, you can never compare anyone to this **Unforgettable Night**.

The Essence of This Woman

Sitting in this class, hoping the time hurry up and past, the door swings open and she walks in, they say beauty is in the eye of the beholder, when I saw this woman I wanted nothing more than to hold her close to my heart, take her by the hand and go far away from here without any worry or cares because I have her near, I fear I'm falling in love and I don't even know this woman what is becoming of me, knowing I can give her what she needs, in my mind I'm saying baby come feed me, let me squeeze you tight, kiss you soft and love you with all my might, each day and every night, closing my eyes seeing nothing, but you when the sun rises at the break of drawn, I'm so fond of this woman, she has me smiling from my soul and she doesn't even know, if I ever had a chance I would never let go, I just need one sign so that I can show her the time of her life, I don't have to think twice, I know I found Miss Right, my Queen to be, with you being in my life is all I can see, looking deep into her eyes to no surprise I become hypnotized, my hands begins to slide up and down her spine, to her hips as I greet her with a kiss, **The Essence of this Woman** has my soul on fire she is my only desire, I plan to seek and conquer her love, her skin is soft like the feathers of a dove, made from heaven above, in love I am with the beauty of this woman, her smile, her walk, the way she talks has me open, from the way she smells ever so sweet to her long black hair and those pretty little feet, she has my body weak, I continue to glance at her just to sneak a peek, she just don't know what she's doing to me, **The Essence of this Woman** has the man coming out of me, opening my eyes to realize it was a fantasy of mine I look back and see this fine divine woman with every man in the room bum rushing at every given chance, she looks directly at me as if I was next in line, but with a smile ever so wide, gathering up enough pride putting my fears and ego aside I walk over to her extending my hand saying my name is King I just had the weirdest dream about you, I was with you and you were with me together forever just the two of us, she smiled and blushed saying that's a crazy rush I just had a dream about you kissing me softly which is a plus, this is love not lust, destined to be together this is a must, trust my thoughts when I first saw you I was saying **The Essence of this Man** I wonder what type of plan he would have for a woman like me, but I was too shy to speak, your swag your smile just had me going wild inside had me thinking about a lifetime ride, wanting to love you deep from within my soul and never let go, I see we have the same thoughts and goals forever together, never letting go of us, this will be a lifetime show, **The Essence of this Woman** has my heart and soul on float, on cloud eleven kissing her softly as we fly off into the heavens.

Love Where Are You

I've been searching for so long, waiting for love to come home, Where is that real unconditional running through your veins and heart deep kind of soul-burning love, that inseparable can't be without you I need you in my life type of love, a special gift sent from above type of love, that I couldn't go through life without your type of love, forever can weather any storm that comes in any form type of love, **Love Where Are You**, *I am missing the things you can do, that can't nobody tell me about your type of love is what I crave will misbehave to keep you in my life type of love, that Valentine's Day every day type of love taking you down showing you I'm not playing around type of love, my number one my only one type of love saying thank you to the heavens as you my angel sing my name when I'm pleasuring you with my lasting endeavor type of love, kissing you until your lipstick is gone type of love you is where I belong type of love, a love so strong a love that will love on past our time our grand kids will talk about our beautiful find, that's keeping my heart pumping kind of love with the passion, fire and desire we have in the beginning staying lit until the end type of love, so real if you had to choose again you will chose me again kind of love, I've been searching high and low, looking for you coast to coast, from a boat to a plane* **Love Where Are You**, *I'm going insane.*

Break You Down

Meeting you in this undisclosed location, time is what we won't be wasting, loving the affection we're displaying, no playing when it comes to you, are you ready to feel what I'm about to do to your perfect body once I pull and push inside it, the way I'm about to **Break You Down**, the way I'm about to put it down will have you skipping work on your knees at church thanking God for this love affair as I spread your wings flying high in the air without a care in the world, let me relax you my girl, put your purse down and take off that jacket, this is an love attraction like no other as I pull back the covers to lay you down on my feather soft pillows, thoughts racing through my mind of being deep in the middle, I begin undressing you from your head to your sexy feet, I love the way you smile at me, from your face to those lips in between those hips and thighs, I stand to undress showing you I'm fully equipped as my passion rises and rises the look in your eyes says it all when I'm gone you will be having withdraws, there's no flaws in the way I'm about to **Break You Down**, you have found a real King let me show you what I mean, as I lay on top our hands and fingers interlock, French kissing nonstop, tongue twisting filled with bliss, kissing you slowly no part of your body will be missed, making sure I touch every inch, my love this is my gift to you as **I Break You Down** with the things I do, my tongue begins to creep down your neck flirting with my hands on your breasts, tonight there will be no rest, I will be putting in overtime you're so fine I'm glad you're all mine, I found myself below your navel in between your thighs as the temperature is raised high, giving you a feeling you never felt before my love, my passion from here on out cannot go on being ignored my knees drop to the floor, I start to explore your candy of love placing no one above, you taste so sweet, you started tugging and clenching the sheets, your legs are shaking becoming weak as my tongue goes in deep around and around moving to the rhythm and beat of our hearts, tonight I'm going to take you far, oh how beautiful you are to me I'm going to give you all of me, coming up slow to give you that royal freak show, kissing you at your feet up your legs pass your thighs to your stomach as I gaze and look you in the eyes real seductive and sexual tonight I'm blessing you sliding into that right place your mouth drops as I fill your space my stokes will take the cake as I shift, move and groove my way, speechless with no words to say, can you handle it as I go there baby with you, tearing you into two, thrashing and smashing in a soft gentle way giving you all my love, lip locking while our bodies popping there's no stopping the way I **Break You Down**, watch what I have in stored for you the next time you come into my town... (To be continued).

A Lifetime

All my days I been looking for you to come my way, a love that is so rare, a love that I can never compare to another, someone who I can bring home to my mother, a love like no other, I will spend **A Lifetime** to find that one defined love, I'm waiting on the heavens above to send her to me, as I seek and seek loving different ones in between my sheets, I haven't found one that I can keep around me for **A Lifetime**, someone I can call all mine for **A Lifetime** spending my life to find that one underneath this sun my heart belongs to that special one, waiting on her I am to come my way and say I am here to stay for **A Lifetime** and even in death our souls will be intertwined for all time I want you by my side giving me your all, there's nothing I won't do for you, whatever you need I will be here to feed you, have no fear my heart belongs to you, waiting patiently for that woman to arrive and come near, even if it takes all my days, **A Lifetime** to find that right one to stand beside me and hold me each and every night, I will wait for that day for that woman to appear and say forever you will be mine for the rest of our lives I will love thee together just you and me, this love can't be defeated, exceeding all my expectations meeting my requirements, I will be waiting **A Lifetime** for you so I can be completed.

Never Ending Love

These words I say to you are true, I will forever be with you, give me your heart and I will show you how far my love can go, let go of your past that fool couldn't last, couldn't see what he had in the palm of his hands, give me a chance to show you **Never Ending Love**, I am your angel sent from heavens above, going hand and hand like a glove, I'm one you will never be able to get rid of, this love, my love you will never get tired of, my beautiful dove I'm about to bring down you walls and exposed the love you've been hiding for years, from deep within I see the fears you have stored inside your soul not wanting to love anymore, let me take control of your heart that has been stuck in time, frozen cold I will forever hold you close with my **Never Ending Love** allow our hearts to beat as one, this love I have for you has just begun, I can't hide it, you have my heart so excited, my soul on fire like the sun, burning and yearning for your touch, never have I felt so much for anyone in my life, I'm ready to spend the rest of my life with you, pleasing you, giving you that real love, something your past relationships couldn't do, looking right through you like an x-ray as I explore I can't bear to see you in pain anymore, I'm signing my name here on the dotted line forever yours, your heart won't hurt anymore, you are the one I will adore from here on out erasing all doubts you have in your mind, it's time you open your wings and fly with me above the skies across the seas, through your lovely eyes all I can see is you and me, this love is times three, there's no others like me, I haven't even talked about what I can do sexually, just know that it's a plus there's no rush, this is not lust, but love from the ground up high, this will be a never-ending ride, your every wish is my command standing side by side loving you the way you need each day and every night, as I feed your soul with this **Never Ending Love** making sure you could never get enough, sending a chill a rush up and down your body, you shouldn't fight this feeling you never felt before I have so much in store, no more being lonely and closing the door on love, let me give you everything you deserve for the rest of your time here on earth, showing you what you are really worth and then some, like I said I've just begun to show you what I can do, the love I have inside of me for you can't be compared, I'm on a different level as I share this **Never Ending Love** with you, giving you the best I will never rest as long as my heart beats within my chest, I'm sincerely yours, no more frowns it's time to see your heart smile from here on out, treating you like a diamond, a jewel my Queen you stand for everything that word means, this is not a damn dream or a fantasy, this **Never Ending Love** is now your reality.

My Spanish Rose

Years ago I had this love that glowed, flowed through my veins, everywhere I go people knew it was you that had me feeling this way without even saying your name, let me explain why **My Spanish Rose** had me going insane, one day taken by surprise by this beautiful face, all it took was one look through your sexy brown eyes that day I claimed you as my prize, you had me hooked, my mind, body and soul were shook, my feelings rose high to another level, love at first sight like a fairy tale from a book, my heart pacing fast, thoughts racing through my mind on how can I make this feeling last, you walked by and gave me a smile that had me going crazy wild inside. I want you in my life, but to shy too say hey my love can I have a minute off your time, a tap on my shoulder from my boy saying conquer that mission every other man here went fishing, but she didn't take their bait, I see that smile on her face you shouldn't wait, but I play it cool and let her leave the room, another time on my time letting her think in her mind she's not the one I want by my side even though her smile brightens up my life, I must keep her guessing why haven't this man come to me after I gave him the keys to approach me, just watch and see one day soon she will be a part of me, raising the stakes everyone on my team throwing money in my face I bet you can't get a date, I laugh and pass on the money and say I will get a date and much, much more she will become my woman and I will forever score, win her love, she is too precious to bet on, like a dove she is God's gift watch how smooth and swift I am, this is real feelings as I seek out my prize that next night on sight I walk up to her asking can we take a walk, can I have a minute of your time, I'm digging your style and the way you move, your smile has me in a different groove can I prove what a man I can be to you, taking my hand she does as I lay my life out on the line, not wasting no time in making her mine, exchanging numbers, oh how did I come to find this tasty wine, feeling me with so much joy inside as we part ways I say have a good game with a hug, her lovely smell is the one thing I remember so much of, this is the start of an incredible love, now I'm holding her in the palm of my hands ready for this life time dance, she's been hurt so bad and I'm the first she gave a chance to, bringing those walls down doing everything I need to do to keep her thoughts off that clown, she falling back in love now, time going past as my love for you remains still, she tatted my name on her back so I know this love is real, I'm giving her feelings her last couldn't give, months passed and we're happy and glad that we found each other the way I love **My Spanish Rose** underneath these covers will never be like no other, I even met her father and mother this love was like no other, but check this twist I'm still young with flaws y'all, my son was just born y'all and that love for my son's mother was still there how can I compare, how can I share my feelings between the two I didn't know what to do, loving the one I'm with, but at the same time I didn't want to be like my father and turn my back on my family can you blame me? In a way you can, why because I let it get deep years go by and I continue to creep between the two, tears pour from both sides even my heart begins to cry no lie we stood outside all night trying to figure this thing out, I couldn't let go of neither one my heart is melting underneath the sun, I had to choose sitting in this meeting between the two, so I chose my family thinking that was the right thing to do as much as I love you I can't leave my son, **My Spanish Rose** says then I know what I need to do with tears in her eyes I will call you with a date and time, if you can't be there then it's fine I will forever love you for the rest of my life, deep down inside I was watching my wife walk out of my life, starting to think twice running after my angel in disguise, grabbing her by the hand saying I want you my love, I want you in my life I'm sorry for what I caused with tears running down my jaws, but wait what about the promise I just made to my son's mother's face, I'm back in the same place... (To be continued).

Never Duplicated

My Queen, my love, my life I put no one else above you, come into my heart and let me show you why I'm so in love with my **Never Duplicated**, I rate you a nine let me explain why, no one is perfect besides God, but in my eyes you're a perfect nine, each and every time you take time to take time to look me in the eyes with your beautiful brown almond shaped eyes, my love rises to another level, my stress goes down another level, the temperature goes up to the roof, kissing you on those soft fully round perfectly shaped lips, your living proof angels do exist here on earth, my baby my girl the woman I will forever adore, share my world, not only when I'm exploring your body it's your mind your spiritual motivation ride or die without question love you professing when anyone tries stepping close to you, plus your patience, (sigh) your patience, I'm honored you saw fit I was worthy enough for you to be patient, professing my love holding you close your arms around me tight as I squeeze and hug you light, my hands come up left and right grabbing you by the face gently, kissing you brings a special joy to my life, for the rest of my days I want you as my wife, my **Never Duplicated** this love will never fade out I have no doubt in these words falling from my mouth, pulling you closer hands falling south to your hips, this passion which burns inside will never quit, I have no problem admitting these feelings to the world my apple head, my boom boom love, these nicknames I play with my *precious dove, only your name comes racing to mind when these words are paired together we can weather any storm my **Never Duplicated** loves me in many different ways and forms it's nothing like the norm, these acts of love she perform gives her the right to wear the crown and sit on the throne, no one else matters to you I belong taking each other's hands as we walk into the King's land, rose petals at the floor as I open the door, your eyes set sights on the bed white roses is the spread covering every inch of the bed, this is my life plan to love you deeply, completely giving you everything I have inside of me, only your love burns inside of me breaking me down and making me weak, to you I surrender waving the white flag for which I am glad to do as we lay holding each other close you're rubbing on my arms and chest kissing me at the neck showing me affection putting my mind on float, closing my eyes as I pull you close and kiss you slowly before falling into this heated act of real love I say, my heart will forever belong to you from deep within my soul, 143, I can never let go of our passion, you continue to show me in a different fashion how love can be given in different actions, so this I say to you is so very true, can't no other woman compete with the essence of you, my **Never Duplicated**.*

Lovers' Land

Welcome to my land of love, with one touch your body will become free, my powers will take over and I will fulfill your every need as I proceed to sweep you off your feet kissing you soft and sweet, showing you things only my love can bring, laying you down gently before I pour us a drink, you give me a wink, I blow you a kiss before I sip handing you your glass, I have x-ray vision I see right through you I'm nothing like your past, this is a love that will never do you wrong you're in the safe comfort of King's arms, my love you will see in many shapes and forms, this loving I will give you is just a plus, you felt my vibe with just one touch of my lips, you giggle and sip standing up to give me a kiss, baby do you know what you do to me? You say, I say yes I bless you with real love, you never felt this good before, your love I will forever explore until the end of time and even then I will somehow come back to find your love again, you smile and say ok you did that you have me now I'm all in, you're a sexy little hottie, stripping down as the words fall out, I'm loving every inch of your body, loving how you left your heels on, see the love I possess makes you perform out of your norm, I bring that real woman out of you, showing you your worth each and every time I explore your earth, your body my palace soft and gentle when I attack it, putting my drink down after another sip, ready to hop aboard this lovers' trip turning back around to find you right in front of me gazing in my eyes, I gaze in yours, you kiss me hard pulling of my shirt I lift you off the floor on this night I will give you something you never felt before kissing with so much passion I'm still holding you high your hips and thighs wrap around my waist, face to face I will erase all pain the others were insane to leave your side, laying you on your back to the bed, licking on your neck rubbing on your legs, relaxing your mind, body and spirit, my love you are about to feel it, my power and how I divide and conquer, moving in between your chest taking my time as I play with your breasts making you hotter and wet, I am your teacher the ultimate test, passing your curves and waist, spreading your thighs wide so I can taste your fruits, you might want to grab that pillow for what I'm about to do, licking your pearl tongue slow my chain hairs give you a little tickle as you let a laugh go, I lick again with my index finger doing circular motions around your palace, your body begins to rock to my groove as I tongue kiss deep inside I have your body boiling hot, you're starting to scream and shout, **Lovers' Land** I am King this is what I'm about picking you up with your legs on my shoulders, your waterfall starts to flowing, I'm giving you more than what you were hoping for, I just begun to explore your body, bringing you down slow, your feet hit the floor my pants fall to the floor, you drop down and say can I even the score, you grab my royal staff with your right hand going back and forth as your tongue begins to explore around and around up and down in and out deep down your juicy mouth without a doubt you're showing me what you're about, curling my toes hands on my head feeling good in **Lovers' Land**, you rise up for a kiss I lay you on the bed and spread your legs, it's time I see those love faces, as I take my place inside your palace, candles burning your body was forever yearning for this day, for me to fill your space, stroking you ever so deeply making sure you feel all of me, biting on your bottom lip you are, I'm about to take your body far, push you to the limits, from beginning to ending I will give you all of me as I continue to creep through your warm walls your hand begin to hit the walls, I interlock both hands putting your legs on my shoulders to do another dance, warning you in advance that I'm about to bring you deep pleasure, my love could never be measured, stroke after stroke my love invokes your body loving the music we are making, undying love you will never be able to get enough of as I take you higher and above the rest, stimulating every part of your body, as I rock you none stop hitting that spot you're ready to cum scratching my back clinching my chest your body goes numb with your love flowing down my royal staff, my legs tighten I begin to show my wrath, you choose the right path to my **Lovers' Land**, falling asleep with you in my hands.

Unbreakable

I have a love that I cannot deny, my love for her is **Unbreakable**, I want no one else, but her by my side, no other woman can penetrate my ice cold walls, my heart lies in her hands, as I close my eyes running through the halls of my mind, I come to find only your beautiful face, a taste of heaven enters my soul when blessed with your grace, I rather not be anywhere else, but here, no need to worry or fear my heart is for you, I will spend my life showing how much my love is true, this is a vow that shall not be broken, a real connection, the way I give you affection, relieving all your stress pleasuring you the best, I will never rest, my love your love will forever beat within my chest, deep down to my soul, this love is **Unbreakable**, I just can't let go, I can't get enough of your love, I'm so addicted to you and the things you do I just can't get enough of you, I am yours forever holding you close my heart won't allow anyone else to get close, we can pour the wine and say a toast, cling the glass and drink, have fun, dance and boast to the limo we go, singing to each other we did it I'm in this until our life's ending, this is just the beginning of this **Unbreakable** feeling with you I'm winning.

Blow Your Mind

As we sip on this wine I want to assure you that you won't need no weed to **Blow Your Mind**, I will be all the drugs you need, I will feed your mind my beautiful lady you're so fine, I'm going to take my time so that you understand that you're dealing with a real man tonight, your body won't be able to fight or resist, I will have you wrapped around my finger in a twist by just one kiss, when I shoot I don't miss, you will be on a forever love voyage trip my love you will never dismiss, close your eyes and picture this, you and I are alone, I'm kissing you slow and soft while rubbing on your thighs making the temperature rise, I am not your natural guy, taking it up a notch as we fly high I'm hitting all your right spots, licking you slow behind your ear, putting all your feelings and emotions in gear a single tear drops from your eye followed by an oh my you haven't even being inside and your blowing my mind, baby let me explain that why, it's the feeling, it's the vibe my love inside comes out when you stand in my sights, especially when we're making love all night, spreading your wings to lick your pearl tongue just right in different positions and ways up and down, by now you should know games I don't play, tonight we will escape as I dash in and out of your secret place, I glance up to get a look of your beautiful face, satisfaction I give I see that can't be erased, passion cries your body going crazy and wild inside my tongue is doing you just right making you smile as I **Blow Your Mind**, your legs are getting tight screaming you're going to make me cum all night, we're off the Remy v as I stand to give you a sneak peek of what I have in between my thighs, just above my knees, the look upon your face says your pleased, blessed I am here to fulfill all your needs I say laying you back kissing you soft before I begin my attack, rain starts to hit the window pain, these feelings you feel are driving you insane as I slide in to take away any pain you may have, I am your first and your last, and what I mean by first is your first real love the ones before me couldn't make you melt with just one touch of the lips, as I continue to stroke in between your hips, what I mean by last, as you feel that I'm well-endowed and fully equipped, any man that steps to you after tonight, they attempt will be killed, shot down why because can't nobody love you like this guy as I **Blow Your Mind** each and every night over and over and over and over again I'm going deeper and deeper within, the room takes a spin and a spin, your waterfall begins to swim and swim all over again as the candles dim you want me to forever live inside, with just one look into my eyes I grant your wish for I will forever **Blow Your Mind**, for all time.

He's Where You are, but I'm Where You Want to be.

It's very unfortunate for how you may feel, the one you're with right now is just games it isn't real, the one you're with doesn't make you feel the way that I make you feel even when I am not near, the very thought of me brings a single tear, I want you here, you want to be here, rip off that stray jacket break lose, release your fear, for with me no hurt, harm or danger will ever be able to penetrate my force field, my mind is focused as I concentrate on nothing, but your love, I'm your gift, your heart just melts when we kiss, you're my star above, I stay up all night just to see you shine and feel your love, we have wasted enough time, I'm texting your phone and ringing your line wanting you to express your feelings you have inside for me to him, how each time you're making love it's me you're thinking of, calling out my name in your head, that's proof your relationship is dead, aren't you tired of hearing him complain, putting you down and making you feel ashamed less than a woman, like each season it's time for a change, where I am is nothing, but good loving, uplifting you high, showing you how a good woman should be treated right, it's time for a new life, break free from the stripes and chains, I'm here to forever change your feelings, so pack your bags I'm on my way, for today will be a new beginning, I'm with you until life's ending.

My Computer Love

*Our conversations are putting me in this groove wanting nothing more than to be with you, using my right and left arrow to scroll and move, I'm so ready to esc this box, come over and show you what I have, I have your stored and your number locked, you're holding down that number one spot as I shift to all caps lock, to let you know I'M HOLDING YOUR HEART DOWN ON MY BLOCK IN MY TOWN I'M IN CONTROL ALL I WANT TO DO IS HOLD YOU CLOSE, wait I don't want to Skype let's be bold, let me come over and down arrow low, I just want to touch you slow, hitting enter to gain access to your soul, after tonight to your friends you will brag and boast, in due time I will be standing at your door, tired of texting it's your body my fingers want to explore, log into your insides and love you more and more, my beautiful love it's you I adore, I knock at the door it swings open and you start kissing me like never before, from the bed to the floor from the floor to the couch, now you're on top to even up the score, I'm deleting all doubt, you're sitting upright, riding me back and forth you start to get loud, stimulating your body my heart I can't hide it, Miss Perfect, waiting for this passion was well worth it, no more web searching and speed dates, flipping you over to fill your backspace, tasting your lips as you look back and say page up and down, go in, F10 I'm about to cum I forever want you **My Computer Love**.*

Pleasing You

I want nothing more than to come into your life and **Please You**, all night I will have you flying high as a kite, it's all about you so sit back and enjoy the ride, take my hand and step into my room of ecstasy where real love will be revealed, I will give you the best of me, after tonight your heart will be forever mine closed and sealed, real love is what you've been yearning to feel, come here and bring your body near I know you have doubts and you may fears, but I promise I will steer your feelings, love and soul in the right directions, I am the best love you can ever know, your heart will be forever protected, satisfaction when we're sexing taking away your pain no more stressing, compressing all those bad memories as I proceed to give you everything you need, fulfilling your every desire, I couldn't squire this chance to devour you in my love nest, **Pleasing You** will be my life's quest, you should never settle for second best, your worth is more you need me a man who can explore your mind and body, you become so excited once I pull inside it, your feelings become uncontrollable these are feelings you never felt before, stabling your mind as I give you more, pushing deep into your inner core, adoring this pleasure as you begin to weather raining down on my sheets, the things I'm doing to your body has you venerable and weak, no other guy can compete with the way I **Please You** in between the sheets.

My Life Commitment

These words I express to you are true, all I want in my life is you, there's no me if it's not you I see waking up next to me or the last thing I see before my eyes close to sleep for eternity, I will do nothing, but breath your love I am blessed to know a love of your stature of your virtue **My Life Commitment** starts with you, showing love in everything that I do, pleasing you without rush I want you to feel each and every touch, no lust in this love, you're a must have in my life no thinking twice about this choice I have made, my plans are laid I want you in the worst way, this promise is about give and take, I can forgive any mistake my love for you is just that great, I don't play when it comes to your grace, nothing, but smiles comes upon my face as my body aches and yearns for you to take your place, my heart and soul rises to the sun when I grab you close and tight around your waist, my feelings shoot through the roof into outer space, this lock I have will never become loose, my feelings, love, heart and soul is my proof, plus my loyalty will be given in everything I do, you can trust right from the beginning this love my love knows no ending, I will be spending the rest of my days living **My Life Commitment**.

One and Only

I can't compare you to the rest, the way you kiss me while rubbing your hands across my chest, you have me in a mess, around and around in circles as you do the most, showing me why you're the one and only, the best, taking me high as I float off into my freaky emotions, thinking of the ways we be coasting, all my friends are roasting because I'm caught up in your love potion, understand this doesn't happen to King let me explain what I mean it feels like a dream, you have me telling my folks how I became a fiend for your love, these are the words I spoke of when expressing my feelings for you, I hope she is my **One and Only**, I have spent enough days of being lonely, I've been longing to share this love I have inside, I declare the rest of you women beware, this love I have for her I will never share, my girl is my world, she is my air, my unbreakable rock, you hit each and every spot from my physical to my mental compelling each thought that comes to my mind, I want to spend a lifetime feeling the way I feel with you by my side, if this love is wrong shit I don't want to be right, from deep inside I will fight to have you in my life, I will prove to you each day and night that I am worthy enough to have you as my wife, my love, my heart and soul no one else comes close to you my beautiful dove, my **One and Only** I am so caught up in your love.

My Vows

The day has come for us to be joined together and become one, you are my heart, my life and after this hour passes you will be my wife, the pastor passes me the mic, I proceed to tell you why this love will love on for the rest of my life, how I will never stop loving you with all my might, break down look at what I have found it has been some long years, you standing here looking so beautiful I can't hold back my tears of joy, for today I will forever be yours and you will forever be mine, I'm marrying my angel who is just right, taking your hand I pledge to be only your man, I vow to love to hold to cherish and never disrespect the love we share, this love will never reach its climax, these are facts for years to come in each and every act I will show you love, giving you reason to never be tired of the passion I possess, putting your left hand across my chest, my heart beat will forever move to the sound of your love I will never rest in giving you my best, but I can be honest I cannot lie, for there will be some real good days, but we will also encounter some bad times, I promise I will never take you for granted or misbehave no other can take your place for I will never find another woman of your grace, you keep a never-ending smile upon my face, you have filled my empty space, sliding this ring onto your finger showing you this love can never be erased, these vows, **My Vows** I will forever say I will love you for the rest of my days.

Perfect in my Eyes

Each day and night I want no one else, but you by my side, **Perfect in my Eyes** you are, my heart is forever yours to explore to hold to cherish, this love can never be buried, it will never perish lasting forever talking over my mind and body, that look you give me is so exotic, you have my feelings so excited, exterminating any thoughts I may have inside for any other, the way you do things when we in between the covers, you are my perfect lover, discovering emotions I thought I've locked away, showing me it's ok to feel this way, you are perfect in every way and so is this love we share, sitting back indulged in my thoughts trying to compare, you have me flying high beyond the skies into a new life mission, you are everything I've been wishing for my love it's you I adore, enter my mind for a while to explore my very thoughts of your love, you are one I could never get rid of, I could never get enough of that pretty smile which moves me and drives me wild, your my greatness gift, to the smoothness of your skin I love to be in, inside of your passion, I've never seen love actions like this, I promise to give you all I have to give for as long as I live, in your eyes I see our present our future and past, by the way you look at me I know this love will last, I hope that one day you will come to realize how perfect you are when seen through my eyes.

Dontae Cottrell

Showdown

I've heard around town that your love could not be brought down, I want you to know your match has been found in me, I am everything you will ever need just watch and see once I open you up and pull in between your knees, your heart will only pump and bleed for my love after I'm done showing you my worth, I am King here on this earth travel the world to find you my woman, my girl, don't defer, take my hand and let me show you the way, it's going to be a **Showdown** *today, forever your love will stay with me as I proceed to do the things that will have you weak, giving you a wink before pulling you close, now you're lying next to me rubbing on my chest your eyes are telling me what you think, never have you been with a man like me and never will you be, one of a kind I am, God only made one me, kissing you soft on your cheek moving to your lips our tongues begin to twist I feel a dip in your hips, your heartbeat takes a skip, your hands feel that I'm well endowed, I will be the only love allowed to flow through your river of love, I want you to see what I'm made of, speechless you are laying closely, you starting to feel the effect of my love potion, my tongue is in motion down your ever glades, I see that you shave sexy I say, before I'm done your love will fall my tongue reaches your walls you start to call out my name, when I'm done you will never feel the same, you will be leaving me with no complaints, I'm doing the most driving you insane, my fingers begin to stroke, my* tongue continues to lick, while your body begins to coast, you're feeling like you're at sea the way I'm rocking your boat, I'm the captain of your ship as I finish my lick with a kiss, my fingers continue to twist and stick, kissing you on your breasts then lips sliding my full equip in between your hips, soaked and wet you are I'm going deep and hard, far inside, no more running your love can't hide, I have arrived to be the man in your life that brings your love wall down, giving you a few more strokes before I turn you around, your eyes are screaming out wow, while your lips are saying oh my God you're so deep inside of me, my legs are feeling weak what is becoming of me, you begin to weep a tear rolls down your cheek, it's me treating you like a woman's supposed to be treated, making real love, blessing you with my gift from up above, flipping you over to give you more love, pulling on your hair soft and gently, spreading you wide so you can feel me deeply, taking over your mental so you feel all of me inside giving you what you need as I proceed you can't hold it no more exploding your love all over me, blooming like a flower your love I have devoured, we have been going for hours, staying fresh my **Showdown** will never go sour, my beautiful dove falling asleep with only me on your mind, I'm the only one you will be able to think of, my touch is just that much.

Dontae Cottrell

Definition of Love

I believe I was put here on earth to show each and every woman what it means to be loved, sex is just a plus that's easy, it's what you show your significant other after that act of passion how much you love her, believe me, showing you will do anything for that one, go beyond and above, this is my gift to you, I am here when that guy acts a fool to listen and be that shoulder you cry on in person or on the phone I will never leave you alone, you can call on King, taking away your pain, let me show you what I mean, let me explain, a woman will allow you to do what whatever you want to do if she is in love with you, but when you take her love for granted it's me she will run to, not for sex that's too easy, but for love believe me, unconditional love, my words will do all the touching and rubbing making her feel so good inside to the point she will forget about the fight she had with you last night, you must adore the one you're with, eye searching each time you're out you better quit, you don't know what problems that next woman will come with, spending all your time to get to know one just to mess up, you better stand up straight, take it from me I lost one true love and every night my heart aches, if only I can go back to that day to correct my mistake I would be with her until this day, there is a price to pay when you're playing with that word love, women take that seriously, that's all they think of, when you find that one who gives you nothing, but good love, you must put away all childish acts, stay where you are and show her love is real, you not out there playing infield trying to unveil some freaky acts with another, your woman should be all the freak you need under the covers, you can't be in a relationship and be single at the same damn time, you will come to find yourself alone in your home wondering what went wrong calling your love on the phone, but she's not answering why because she will be with me, I will be giving her all she needs and much, much more, picking up your pieces putting her heart back together again, there's magic in my hands my love will forever stand intact, this is a fact I will never be back in the place you are at, I have learned what it means to truly love a woman, from deep down in my stomach to my soul, I have the tools to show and prove this is what a broken heart will do to you, this is true, it will open your eyes to see the real **Definition of Love** take it from me don't place nothing or no one above.

Dontae Cottrell

Co-Star

Welcome to my auditions, if I feel you're worthy enough then you will have the position, show me you can be submissive in this wild freaky scene you are on a mission, to show and prove to your lover you are everything he will ever need underneath these silk covers, an action, you walk in ready to please and give satisfaction, with nothing, but your heels, bra and your lace thong on, telling me to hang up the phone, handing me a drink while you light and puff my cigar before you pass it to me, I say what did I do to deserve this treat, you reply with the love you give me inside I felt I should give you a little surprise, up and down my eyes go, looking at those thighs I'm ready for your rodeo show as I drink and smoke you turn on some music to dance slow, my body begins to float, high I go from the smoke, this drink is hitting me low, you will know what I mean when you feel my stroke, your body looks so good the way you're coasting and moving I'm loving what you're doing showing and proving, grooving to the rhythms of love, taking my hand standing me up, telling me first we're going to take it slow and gentle, then it's going to get rough and hard, I want to feel you deep take my mental far, you're the main attraction, I'm just your **Co Star**, kissing slowly, touching low, all over each other here we go, push me down to the bed climbing on top licking behind my ears hitting my spot, my passion is raising nonstop, kissing on my chest passing my abs below my waist, look at what you have staring you in the face, you begin to give me a taste, a lick followed with a kiss to my tip, making me want to tap and quit, curling my toes, my eyes are closed as you continue to work me down below, my expression shows you feels so good, I'm hard as wood, you would take it all if you could, with the things you're doing to me I should write a book, my feelings and emotions are shook, I see you're trying to have me trapped and hooked, still going soft and gentle, this day and night will be unforgettable, as you stand sliding off your thong grabbing and kissing me slow, putting me in a place where I belong, your palace is so wet and warm, you begin to perform riding me nice and slow, making love to my never-ending stroke, deep in I go and go, around and around as your head float backwards, I'm all that matters right now, when in your town, you're going up and down picking up speed giving me what I need, I feel you getting weak, I'm gripping your cheeks as you bounce on top of me, exploding you are times three, you say that was the soft and gentle way take control my love and give it to me the hard way, I sit up and say the way we're going we will be making a baby today, believe what I say can't nobody do your body the way I can, your love is raining down slow like quicksand as we stand I push you up against the wall kissing you hard, in these arms I have strength I won't let you fall, swimming through your halls I heard the law, but they're not coming for us you're in luck as I make you bust and bust uncontrollably, looking deep into your eyes seeing that your falling in love with me, caring you over to the bed where there is more passion to be made, feeding you more and more holding your legs back, before I attack I show you what my tongue can do, wet you are, how far will you allow me to go, you will win an Oscar for the show you're giving, best supporting actress, holding tight on to my mattress, while my tongue is licking showing satisfaction, I rise to begin my attacking, your legs on my shoulders while your nails are back scratching going deep into your love palace with each stroke, hard is my waves as I crash up against you with my hands around your throat, you're moaning begging for more driving you crazy as I explore your insides oh what a night we're having, transitioning into another position before we cut and are finished, standing you up turning you around to show you what you have been missing, you bend over touching your toes, showing me that smile below, touching my soul as I slide in with a long and deep stroke hard and fast a slap to your ass while I dash and thrash, you turn and look back at the way I'm grooving and moving through your body, deep, deep inside it, throwing it back you are shouts and scrams of your taking me far, cut and scene, I'm happy to give you the job, welcome to the team.

Because of You

Because of You my world is now complete, you bring me a joy inside that I just cannot deny, **Because of You** my passion, my love has taken on a new life, down a different path, you are my better half, **Because of You** I know this love will last beyond my days, I love to escape through your eyes **Because of You** my love will forever stay in the abundances of your heart no matter where you are just look up and you will see my love shining brighter than the stars, **Because of You** I am now whole, **Because of You** I can release the love I have buried deep down in my soul, **Because of You** my heart is no longer cold, but warm the way you show love in the ways you perform, **Because of You** I am now wide open, transformed by your love potion, **Because of You** I will forever be coasting across the seas, floating high above the clouds, **Because of You** I have what I need, you bring happiness to me each time that you smile, **Because of You** I am stronger now, no more living free and wild, **Because of You** coming into my life showing me what love is all about, **Because of You** I have no worries or doubts, these words I will forever speak from my soul past my heart through my mouth, I have found my soul mate, my wife, I will go to the highest mountain and scream these words with all my might, for the rest of my life I will understand what it means to be in love, **Because of You** my beautiful dove.

In the Middle of Your Love

*My love I live just to feel your touch, sending a rush up and down my body when I'm **In the Middle of Your Love**, inside you I just can't get enough of, some people may say it's lust, but I disagree I'm in love with the way you show your ever care when we take there, my feelings become so aware when you're near, strapping on my gear before climbing in between our sheets, forever you and me we will be, looking deep into your eyes before I kiss you, bringing a joy to my soul that I cannot explain, having no issue when I'm in your grace, your hold on my heart has forever changed the way I make love, taking my time there's no rush, I want to make sure I don't leave a spot on your body untouched, from your head to your feet, let me show you what I mean, kissing your frontal lobe assuring you I will never let you go, I even kiss your nose with my nose rubbing cheeks, yes we're that close, moving slowly towards your lips ready to take this everlasting trip, as we kiss and kiss our tongues twist, grabbing my ears you are with my hands on your hips, you're biting on your lips when I suck on your ear moving near your neck with a lick there and there making sure I touch you everywhere as I take you higher suspended in the air, my love you cannot be compared, no one has ever made me make love the way I make love to you I swear, holding your breasts close as I lick and suck on them both, your eyes are closed, your feelings are on float and I've just begun to give you a royal show, moving slow* like a snake with my tongue down your stomach around your navel, your body will be taken once I go below your waist showing you that I am able and capable in making it rain and I'm not talking about money or what hits your window pain, I'm talking the feeling that drives you insane making your legs shake, while my tongue flirts and plays with your pearl tongue, hot you are like the sun, in a minute you will be busting like a gun, uncontrollably, just watch and see, sixty seconds pass and now you're feeling weak with the covers on top me, underneath I am between the sheets with your hands massaging my head, kissing you softly on your thighs and legs, even at your pretty little feet, yes I am your love freak, giving your body what it deserves, my love is free, but I wish I can give you the earth, showing you what your worth, I'm putting in overtime you will be skipping work, as I work your body right, all through the night, coming up from being down in these sheets to give you more of me, filling your palace with my royal pipe, holding you tight, a soft bite to my shoulder as I slide back and forth, pulling you closer, south and north between your hips, our lips going east and west, your breasts to my chest relieving your stress our sheets are a mess, the sun is coming up and I just can't get enough, when **In the Middle of Your Love.**

Honest Love

Allow me to set the record straight, there's nothing like **Honest Love**, when the love is honest nothing can go beyond or get between it, every word you say to your love you will mean it, no deception without question your love will be the only love your sexing, **Honest Love** brings out the best from the inside out, when looking into your eyes I have no doubt that the words that surface from your mouth are true, **Honest Love** is perfect no hiding the wrongs putting it all out on the table so that forever we will belong into each other's arms, no reason to sneak and go into each other's phones or even wonder when your love is out and your alone, **Honest Love** will bring your love right back home, when push comes to shove **Honest Love** stands strong, steady and firm, I've learned to always be true and your love if their love is real will always be true with you, if not the dark will come to light, skeletons will be uncovered from being buried because you have **Honest Love** buried in your heart, on **Honest Love** you can go far become married to your love from Venus, **Honest Love** is art, beautiful when painted with the touch of love and blessed from the heavens high above the clouds, Honest Love will not allow no other love to come in between your love, **Honest Love** warms your heart from being cold, grabbing a strong hold that can never be let go, true to its testament, can't be bent or broken, flattered, but unchanged by flirtation words that are spoken by the next you could bet, your **Honest**

Love *will become tested, it's up to you to show that your **Honest Love** is invested in the one you love, in the one you gave your heart to, your everything, the one you don't want to lose, each day you will show and prove how **Honest Love** can make you do things you thought you would never do, like saying no to the woman standing outside your door, willing and ready to explore your acts of love, pressure coming from all angles, up and down, around and around, with **Honest Love** there only can be one in your town to share this special gift with, your mind will flip having you doing anything for the love you're with, **Honest Love** will have you on missions deleting all competition, no more clubs and fishing, you at home cleaning up and washing dishes for your Mrs. Right, **Honest Love** will have your heart flying higher than some kites, jumping through hoops, climbing mountains, breaking down pillars with all your might, signing your name on the dotted line, you will come to find yourself happily married with your **Honest Love**, giving a lifetime commitment, just close your eyes and vision, if there were no honesty in love, do you think you will found that one you can spend the rest of your life with, or will you come to found yourself in and out of different relationship, this thing called **Honest Love** is a trip, get with the program or stay on that sinking ship.*

Dontae Cottrell

Love in the Shower

Driving home from a long day of work, all I can think about is my baby boom, how I want to consume the inside of your womb and the freaky things I want to do, I forget about the world when I'm next to you, taking away my stress you do, your smile brightens my day, holding you close all night puts me in another place, pulling up to our home turning off my phone, don't want to be bothered by any noise, I only want to hear your voice, your lips and kisses are juicy and moist, putting my key into the door saying baby I'm home, but no answer came to my ear, walking back to our room where I see steam and light, with your silhouette looking just right through the glass door, undressed I become as I enter saying I'm home and I'm all yours, having a little conversation before I explore, asking how my day went you are, long and hard as usual, but it's ok now I'm home with you ready to please you in ways you want me to, placing your hands on my back with a towel washing me down, your hands come around to my chest, moving slowly past my waist, your hands take place grabbing my royal, stroking me as you say turn around and kiss me, pivot and turn I do, grabbing you by the face gently kissing you ever so softly, with water running down washing this soap up off me, moving from your lips to your neck, you kiss my chest before dropping down to your knees to please me, loving the way you feel with the shower raining on top of me, taking me deep in and out your mouth, making me weak, forever and ever I'm complete with you next to me, pulling you by your arms so that I can perform kissing you more and more as the wetness pour and pour, your back against the wall, someone is knocking at the front door, never mind them it's your body I'm about to adore, with one leg up as I score, sending my rocket into your outer space, I need more room let's take this to another place, opening up the shower door I'm thinking about pulling you to the floor, but I change my mind grabbing at your waist to raise you high as I pull inside giving me delight as you bounce and ride, I lay you on the bed with your legs to the chandelier before I enter your stratosphere, no whispers, but shouts to my ear the time is near I'm about to cum my love you're hitting all spots as I shift gears speeding down your highway of love, leaving you speechless with no words to say, it's written all over your face your palace will forever be mine for the rest of your days here in this world, blowing your mind, my girl, chills down your spine, as I lay at your side to pull inside, lifting your leg high, turning your face to me to look into your eyes, my love will follow you into your dreams when you sleep, loving you I will for life, kissing you soft as I bust inside, holding you close and tight, as we fall to sleep into each other's arm for the rest of the night I love the way we perform.

The Key to My Love

Throughout my life I been searching for that one I can settle down with, someone I can call my wife, spending the rest of my days with you imprinted on my heart, my love is a blessing from up above, you won't come across a love of my kind, I have a love that is hard to find, so forgive me if I just don't open up my heart to you, my lady you must show and prove that you are down, show me that you hold **The Key to My Love** *to forever stay around, your love has to be forever true, can you enter my life and rule at my side, do you have the tools to make me fall deeply in love with you over and over again each and every night, can you make me do the unthinkable, is it possible, will you forever fight for what I have stored inside, show me that this feeling is right, make me surrender to your sweet tenderness, is your love outta sight, can you be patient as I take my time until I come to find it's you and you alone that I need in my life, I want to give* **The Key to My Love** *to you, but I must know if this is true, I've been hurt so many times before, left alone in the cold, tell me you will never let go when the wind blows, that forever and all times you will be here to shower me with your love, promise to never go back on a promise, show me honest love and you will be my everything, giving you anything your heart desires, your skeletons will show if you're a liar, come into my life and fuel my fire, ignite my soul, my love is frozen solid cold, unbreak my heart and make me warm, show me you're not like the* norm, forever hold me close to your heart, my love is priceless art, you cannot buy my love, for it is a gift that must be given by me if you worthy let me see, looking deep into your eyes I have yet to see a lie that lies inside, you will forever be mine and I'm forever yours to love and cherish, adore this present that I am giving, I want to explore what I have been missing, real love, a love that is strong, good love, a love that will live on and on past our days here on earth, our kids' kids will talk about the way our love was a gift, how two people took vows and never allowed anyone or anything enter our life and destroy the love that we have shared how no one else can be compared, playing it like a grown man ought to, before I lay you down and court you, I want to get to know you, giving you one shot to win my love you better be able to make me fly high and above, tell me if I'm asking for too much, can our hearts become one, when you touch me will chills take over my body, do you have the recipe to give me what I need and keep me excited for what's to come, please tell me are you that one, so I can forever place **The Key to My Love** in your land, I want to know what are your plans to keep me in your hands.

Dontae Cottrell

Can I Make Love to You?

In so many ways, I can make you my love slave, once you enter my room, my cave, my loving impression will live on in your mind for days, let me explain, better yet allow me to take your hand and show you what I can do, leading you to my room of ecstasy, sitting you down on the bed as I pour us a drink, lighting candles as I give you a wink, your mind doesn't know what to think as I sit close next to you, it's about to get sexual, your feelings are what I want to get to know, are you ready for an unbelievable show, all it takes is just one French kiss to have you on a forever trip, my love you will never dismiss, watch this, taking your glass from your hand setting it on the night stand, my lips land on your lips kissing you with passion, the love I give is a different type of action, satisfaction will be given, our tongues are twisting, showing you what you've been missing, taking you on a mission French kissing your neck, pulling off your shirt, I'm about to put in some work, your body will be doing the jerk as I flirt with your breasts unsnapping your bra, standing you up so I can lift you up showing you my strength, we continue to kiss and kiss, this will be a night that you will never forget with your breasts on my lips and my hands around your hips, my royal tongue will be your gift as I lay you down spreading you wide pulling off your pants so that my tongue can go inside, you're giving me that sexy look with your eyes, I can see that I caught you by surprise, the body doesn't lie as you move and groove when I touch your thighs with a kiss, can you handle my freakiness, taking this to the next level digging you out with my tongue like a shovel, making your love rain down, marking my bed with puddles as you cuddle my pillow to your face, letting out screams as I fill your empty place, you're loving these actions that I take, my love can never be replaced, for heaven's sake you shout, I'm coming up with your wetness around my mouth, all smiles and erasing all doubts, as I climb about, finding myself on top of you, unlocking your love with a kiss as I fly right down to your soul, filling your dark hole with my royal pole, holding me tight you are never letting go, taking you far I am, it's all about you and the love we share, sliding in and out with deep strokes, making sure you don't go nowhere, provoking your love with so much care as we stare into each other's eyes, the temperature is on the rise through the roof to skies past the clouds, you're sounding like and owl screaming out oh and ah baby don't stop, you're hitting all my spots making me cum nonstop, time is flying as I peek at my clock, tic-toc, tic-toc, your insides are feeling warm and hot, continuing to make love to you while on top, showing you that my love can never be stopped, rubbing my fingers through your hair, I could never be compared as I vanish off into thin air, you're waking up asking yourself was King really here.

Dontae Cottrell

I Can't Get Enough of You

My eyes show the obvious when kissed by your lips, each and every feeling inside of me is touched, not one is missed when our tongues begins to twist, but that just the tip of the iceberg, stroking my fingers through your long and wavy hair on down to those sexy curves, it's hard for me to put into words why **I Can't get Enough of You**, *through my actions you see I show and prove the way you make me feel is unreal, your smile brings me a great deal of joy, my love has been deployed, it's time that I destroy my past hurts and reveal how my heart really feels, I want this to work, I begin to spill these words to the one I belong to on this earth, forever share my world my love I know your worth, giving you my all, your beauty has brought down my gates and walls, I feel ten feet tall when your inside my arms, showing me love in the warmest regards, without you I go through withdrawals, strung out and all, my love only calls out for you, this is true,* **I can't Get enough of You**, *what am I to do, you complete me, look through my eyes and go beneath me, inside my heart to my soul, it will show your love has an hold on me that I will forever cherish and treasure, my Cherie Amour, this love, our love could never be measured, my heart is forever yours, lasting on and on through those great summer warm days, right past those bad stormy rainy nights, I will continue to love deep down through your tunnel where there goes no light, your love making is outta this world, this I know,* no other love has ever come close to the way you rock it low, loving you with all my strength and might, belief and trust, our love play is a plus, under the covers you like it rough, I'm talking leg ties and cuffs, sending chills up your body while giving you a rush down low when I touch and stroke, you can believe in my quote, **I Can't Get Enough of You** and that is no joke, our hearts are one, forever holding you close, my greatest love underneath the sun, I am a bullet locked and loaded in your gun, waiting for you to pull the trigger, we're Bonnie and Clyde it can't get any realer, for you I will always deliver, no need for doubts and reconsiders, you are my perfect figure, I love it when the seasons turns to winter, I get to hold you close the whole month of December, each day and night I remember, kissing on every inch, every part of your body, until your temperature was brought down, my love is not running any more or hiding, I have finally found an angel who can make my heart smile.

Phenomenal King

Come take a trip through my mind, and you will come to find out why I am King, **Phenomenal King**, I am everything that words means, ruler on high especially when in between your thighs, making your passion rise, setting your soul on fire, taking it up a notch, maybe it's what I'm worth and what I have, that makes me King, **Phenomenal King** I am everything that word means, from the strides in my walk, to me wrapping my arms around you lightly and kissing you softly, taking off your shirt and unveiling your bra, getting you in the mood, you finding stimulation with all my clothes removed as you explore my body in the nude, I'm feeling your body too, nice and tight in all the right places I am ready to show you what I can do, your lips saying damn, could this be, is it for real, is this reality, yes I have skills, Phenomenally I will have your mind thinking of no one, but me, **Phenomenal King**, you will come to learn that I am everything that word means, turning you into a fiend when I kiss you with my drug, your body becomes unplugged, making you fall deep in love with the way that I talk, you thought real love could never be caught, true love will never cost, temptation is warming your insides, setting your heart to defrost when my Phenomenal tongue begins to spark your body start to bend and arch, bringing you into the light out of the dark, I want you to see me in action, I'm a piece of art, poetry in motion, your insides I will be costing with each stroke, the word you will be calling out is Phenomenal, my oral is unstoppable, once my passion enters your soul, deep into you I will continue going, my imaginations are flowing, **Phenomenal King** is the only one you will be knowing, closing your eyes now you're floating on a cloud, as I push inside making you scream wow, it's been hours, it's been a while, keeping that same smile, you're loving my groove, you're loving my style, **Phenomenal King** will always drive you wild, taking you higher and above, this love stays hot never cold or mild, my love never comes foul, breaking you down every time you come around, a **Phenomenal King** is what you have found, trumpets and horns sounds when I enter your town, blowing your mind, never will I waste your time, satisfying your every need, your feelings shooting from your head past your knees, each time you come into contact with me, I will show you what that word means, I am a **Phenomenal King**.

Putting Your Expectations to Rest

It's finally your turn to have a showdown with the King, oh you're going to learn why I am everything that word means, allow me to set the mood, let me set the scene, the talk around town has your Expectations on high, wondering what is it about this guy that has all the women going crazy over one night, is his love game that tight? Questions you are asking yourself, could he be Mr. Right, you're thinking about the love faces we will be making all night, while overhearing a group of women speak of my delight at the beauty shop on how I made their bodies come alive, when I was on top pushing inside, from that day forward you had me in your mind, in your sights, the first time we met I had your passion on rise with my flirtatious words gathering a mental picture from your beautiful face to your sexy curves that's hugging your waist line, giving you my card with an address, number and time, speechless you come to find yourself as I walk off with a kiss to the right side of your cheek, no need to search anymore, the greatest lover you seek is right here to pleasure your P, you're trying so hard not to show it, but I can tell you wanted me to know it, through your eyes your feelings started flowing, twinkling and glowing, not knowing I will be exceeding all your Expectations no time will be wasted, forever you will be craving my love, I hear a car pull up, as I put the finishing touches on, spraying my body with Dior cologne, it's about to be on, turning off my phone so there's no interruption while I perform, tonight it's you I belong to, your wish is my command, I want nothing more than to please you, my doorbell rings, I wait a second, taking a few puffs of my cigar thinking about how fine you are opening my door, your beauty I do adore, your smile brings me warmth, your body I can't wait to explore, as I welcome you in taking your coat, your curves is nothing like the norm, I pour us a few drinks of that ace of spades before I start to perform, loosening you up, I will make you misbehave, turning you into my love slave, taking your hand leading you to my royal cave, where you find rose petals laid at your feet, my lips move toward your cheek, pulling you closer to me, it's your lips I seek, kissing you soft, bringing back whatever feelings you may have lost, sitting you down on the bed while I remove my shirt, off I go exploring your earth, erasing any pain or hurt, my tongue is about to do work, spreading you low as I start to coast through your tunnel of love, one lick two lick three lick four, you going berserk screaming out more and more, as my knees hit the floor, I'm pulling you closer to the edge of the bed, pushing your knees towards your head with your legs spread wide so my tongue can pleasure your insides, taking you for an enjoyable ride, licking you up and down, massaging your pearl tongue as I go around and around, side to side I look up to find a tear roll from your eyes, this is love I'm giving you tonight, relieving your stress taking you away from all the mess, your love begins to squirt hitting my chest, standing up pulling off my pants to become fully undressed, you haven't seen nothing yet, check my love intelligence, I was heaven sent to you to fulfill your ever desire, I hold the power in between my waist, looking deep into your eyes kissing you slowly on the lips with my hands rubbing on your thighs before I take my place inside your palace, this will be an action to remember, my birthday lands in September, Virgo baby, romance, love and satisfactory is guaranteed to be given and showed, your heart will forever hold a place for me, as I creep in between your knees giving you all of me, going deep and gentle, making sure I hit ever spot so when you leave there's no issue, freaking you with the way I groove and stroke, my love is no joke, my feet set firmly on the floor as I pick you up to give you more, making love in the air, my love is nothing you can prepare for, you're screaming out lord as I perform taking my time with you my beautiful nine, after tonight I will be constantly on your mind, when you are in need I'm the one you will come to find, my love you will forever seek, screaming out King you're making me weak, I can feel you deep, as I lay you down to sleep, forever **Putting your Expectations to Rest** about the one they call King.

Who am I?

Dontae and King are the same person, but you will never catch the two in the same room at the same time look deep into my eyes and you will come to find I'm what you've been needing in your life, you won't think twice after tonight my loving is just that right...... Who am I right now can anyone tell me Dontae or King?, have you ever felt my stroke, have I ever licked in between, from that smile upon your face I can tell that I have touched your heart in a major way, I ask you again with these words I say...... Who am I right now, which one is it that brings a smile to your heart, King or Dontae, through my eyes you can tell that I am here to stay, in different ways I will show you love until my dying day, hurt I am when tears are rolling down your face, I say unto you again my love....... Who am I right now, which one is it that shows his softer side, taking you to a place where his feelings don't hide, am I Dontae or King, has there ever been a Queen worthy of me, will I ever find my rose or will I forever be alone, losing confidence I don't, give me one night and you won't see a need to leave my side, the way I push inside when inside gripping your thighs, you're closing your eyes, each time you take flight on cloud nine, I ask you again....Who am I right now, King or Dontae, I will leave you speechless with no words to say, back breaking while love making taking your pain away, sexual conversation as I love you in different languages, angels do exist, my love you cannot resist, when I touch your lips with a kiss, I never make any mistakes when I take my place inside going at a steady pace, blowing your mind, I ask you again to close your eyes and imagine, Who am I, Dontae or King, your passion rises high when I begin my actions, giving your body satisfaction, down below you start to show a reaction, kissing you softly with passion, my love is everlasting, with each second that is passing you're forgetting about your last, I will outdo your past, I have to ask again before we get to the end, Who am I, King or Dontae, I make up the rules when we play in my room, you will forever want to stay, sweeping you off your feet like a broom your love I will always consume, I'm never rude, I respect everything about you, my heart forever belongs to you, there's nothing I won't do for you, my love is true, I say to you for the last time Who am I, look deep into my eyes and you will come to find Dontae and King are the same person, but you will never catch the two in the same place at the same damn time.

My Royal Party

Welcome to **My Royal Party**, it's about to get naughty, from the look in your eyes I see that your excited, so check my flow as I go and go kissing you slowly your heartbeat picks up its coast as I float from your chest to in between your thighs, taking your passion to another level, raising high through the roof past the starlit skies, closing your eyes to no surprise a loud scream comes from inside while I'm inside pushing you to the limit, I'm not finished until you're finished my love will never deplete, everlasting never ending, this is just the beginning as I continue swimming deep into your palace of love with my tongue, a wet and sticky face is what you see when I come up from pleasuring you in that right way, glancing at your beautiful face as I begin to slither between your waist your heart begins to race my in-and-out action is at a steady pace, embracing all of what you have to give, you were made from my rib, forever this love will live on and on, to me your heart belongs, King of your throne, pushing deep inside, hitting spots that were unknown to your past, putting your legs on my shoulders, welcome to my rollercoaster, grabbing my phone hit rejection on their ass, no need for interruptions while I have your body exploding and busting, erupting all over the place, loving you the way you need, giving you what you feign, I'm your drug in your veins chasing away your pain, as you call out my name I start to pick up my strides pushing inside deep before I come out you scream and shout, picking you up at the hips, wrapping your legs around my waist kissing your lips fighting my grip, I'm about to flip the script before this trip is over allow me to put you down, I want you to turn around and bend over nice and slow bounce and drop it low spreading you wide deep inside I go rocking your boat, stroke after stroke making your river begin to flow, taking you to another level as we float I coast massaging your back with my tongue pleasuring your palace with my desert eagle gun, with long and deep everlasting strides, you turn your head around from the look in your eyes love is evolving inside, your heart I will forever keep this love is no lie, forever you and me crossing your mind, only time will tell as I dwell in your pleasure my love making could never be measured, grabbing at your hair putting that arch in your back as I perform my final attack, giving you every inch of me as you throw it back gripping tight at your waist going at a faster pace, my royal pole begins to stiffen inside your kitten shooting out the gate like a horse in a race, with kisses to the side of your face rolling to your lips expressing my satisfaction with all the love we just made, unleashing me from my cave, one year from this day I will be waiting patiently to see your face again, my love starts and ends with you, every year on this very special day I will show and prove how much I love you.

My Wonderland

Each and every time I enter your mind you drift off into **My Wonderland**, no other man can even come close to what I can do to you or how I make you feel, this love is real, my love making skills puts your heart over the top, never will I stop or cease to give you all of me, closing your eyes thinking about that first time I made your passion rise to no surprise I rocked your body all night, that night making you feel just right, taking you to another level, each and every time I enter your mind, no this is not lust, but love forever mine, this love was designed, destined to be together just you and me, my love has set your soul on fire satisfying your every desire taking you higher than ever before, oh how I do adore and cherish your love putting no one else above, tonight we won't be using a glove, I want to fill you up with a blessing from above my beautiful dove, I see I have you wide open, no more of all that wishing and hoping, I am him, the King you have been waiting for to bring your heart out of the cold forever I will hold your love close to mine never will you find yourself alone again with me you will always win, for I was sent here to love and please only you, doing things you're not used to, I repeat can't no one do it like I do in **My Wonderland** I am King and you are my Queen dropping down to my knees just to please you with my tongue making you burn hot like the sun with your palace flowing like a river each and every time I will deliver, making your body quiver and shiver squeezing tight with your thighs as my tongue goes deeper inside making your body come alive after years of being deprived, your King has finally arrived taking my time as I stand to unbuckle my pants giving you a little dance as you glance up I'm ready to fill you up, overflowing your cup, this didn't happen by accident, this is not luck, but you're in luck as I grip your thighs pulling you towards the edge of the bed spreading your wide so your palace can be fed with my pleasure D, making you feel complete each and every time I stroke you deep, forever I will seek your love my precious love I see what I have done to you, bringing out that freak in you each and every time you think about **My Wonderland**, interlocking our hands as I stand with your legs wrapped around my waist picking up the pace, this is a lifetime race with no ending this is only the beginning, opening your eyes to come an find you were daydreaming the whole time... (To be continued).

Our Conversation

A candlelight dinner set for two, my love I want nothing more than to be inside of you, but first let's set the mood tell me what's on your mind, talk to me as I pour you a little more wine, my King you mean everything to me, when we are apart that's when I miss you the most, tell me how you feel when we are not close? My Queen you have my heart on float past the clouds, it drives me wild how I can close my eyes and picture your smile which brightens up my day, sitting here staring at your face as you fix your lips to say, I am walking on water because of you it's the things you do which make me feel the way I do, taking another sip before these words leave my lips, my love no more of you feeling blue this is true these are facts my heart belongs to you I love everything about you, before I can get the next words out you move closer and say when I love I love hard, with you I have let down my guard, baby my King please do not hurt me, you deserve me and I deserve you, putting my finger across your lips as I flip the script, this is a lifetime trip, I want you forever close, this love our love I will never let go, for your words are true, you deserve me and I deserve you, I wouldn't know what to do if I didn't have you, am I strange for feeling this way so fast? Only a few months have passed, please say forever you will stay, moving in closer you are to say forever I am yours to have and to hold, my heart that once was cold is filled with warmth and joy, baby boy you are what I need

I'm giving you my plea, I promise to cherish you every hour and never let this love devour, grabbing you by the hand while looking you in your beautiful brown eyes forever I will be by your side, I am here to conquer your heart and soul, protecting you from any hurt and harm no need to be alarmed when wrapped in my arms, I will always and forever keep you warm, I'm nothing like the norm, a different breed, stick around this is real love you have found, sweeping you off your feet, this love hasn't begun to peek, I think about your love and I start to weep your heart I will keep close to mine the woman in you I will never find again in this lifetime, with a tear rolling from your eye your my lifelong partner my soul mate my King my everything you have my heart singing loud and screaming proud, these tears I cry are tears of joy I finally have a man and not a boy, with my thumb I wipe away your tears letting you know there's no need to fear a man I am indeed, you're all I need I will be your shoulder to lean on stepping up to your plate catching what you pitch I will never switch my loving will never cease I want ever quit or flip the script, I can't wait to be in between your hips filling you up with heaven's gift, you and I on this journey on a forever trip, I love the taste of your luscious lips when we kiss, pulling me closer to whisper this, when we kiss I feel the strong passion of love, I can't wait to see your love faces when I'm giving you my loving, a little baby will be forming in my oven our lives will be complete, because now we're a family baby you make me so happy, I have no doubt that it is you I am supposed to be with, my love will never quit I become sick when I can't have you near you have erased all fears bringing down my walls I am yours with open arms, I pull you close now we are hugging and kissing slowly as I raise my glass to make a toast to us, yes you are the woman I've been yearning for, yes you are the woman I've been searching this earth for, it's you I adore from here on out I will scream and shout for the world will know I have no doubt in this woman I have found completion, your love I have been seeking, now that you are here in my reach, I'm ready to drop down to one knee praying you will have me for the rest of our days... (To be continued).

Tic-Toc Tic-Toc

My love for you is true, the things you do can't be compared, I need you like I need air to breath, your love breaks me down to my knees all I want to do is please you, put you in my love groove just to watch you move slowly on top hitting each and every spot as the clock Tic Toc Tic Toc, I will be going deeper into your pleasure spot nonstop, filling your palace up as I attack slow, you're loving my coast, kissing you gently, my rhythm has you on float as we switch positions you have me standing at full attention not to mention my heart is overflowing with the desire to love you and only you, watch what I do as I flip you over to massage your neck and back with my tongue before I spread your eagle and hit you with my shotgun, explosive this night will be, Tic Toc Tic Toc no need to worry about the clock we will be going into the sun comes up, spreading your cheeks to push in deep slapping your butt making you scream out King give it all to me, I aim to please I won't be finished until you tap, until you quit, you're loving the way my stick shift moves inside of you putting you in this love groove, I want nothing more than to prove I am the best thing under the sun, this best man in this land on this earth, flipping the script, changing positions, putting you up against the wall to show you my worth, oh how I adore your body you have me so excited can't wait for you to ride it, but first let me lift your leg to my shoulder so I can pull inside it, exploring your body to the core, every twist and turn I yearn more and more for your love, pressing your hands high above our heads, looking deep into your eyes as I kiss and push inside, these feelings I cannot hide, I come alive when inside of your love you are my angel from above, I think I'm falling in love, Tic Toc Tic Toc, nonstop as I pull you to floor now you're on top showing me what you've got, what you have, you plus me that's easy math, as you begin to slide down my royal staff, I can tell from the look upon your face that I am taking you to another place higher than outer space into another region, I have you feigning for my love, this drug of mine you could never find anywhere else, passion is what I deal, like a full course meal plus desert I know your worth as you start to go berserk in your reverse cowgirl, my love is in a twirl, the room is spinning, this night slash morning is coming to its ending as you explode down my royal pole gripping my legs tight with all your might as I fill a stiffness ready to finish this, this love our love is uplifting us higher than the clouds, I'm in awe I'm like wow look what I have found my Queen to be Tic Toc Tic Toc in due time we will see if this was really meant to be.

Dontae Cottrell

Erase Your Pain

It's only me who can save you from this pain, let me try to explain, I know I am the man on the outside looking in, but my feelings I can't hide any longer, it's my shoulder you cry on when he doesn't come home, texting and calling when we can't be alone, I don't know how much longer I can hang on, sitting back waiting on that day you come home where you belong, does he touch you the way I do? I give you what you fiend each and every time you call my line, but with time my feelings have grown from like to love, it drives me insane to see you in pain and you're not even his main, but yet you remain at his side, sneaking out late nights so that I can fulfill your every desire you have hidden inside, through your eyes I see the your heart locked away in a cold place, forever I will stay, bless the day you leave that pain and become my main, he doesn't touch you like this as I take the friction from your lips, my love will forever take you on a passion trip, loving you the way you need with no one to stop us, being the drugs in your veins fighting through your pain loving you the way you need I can't stress that enough, the love I have in store for you is a plus, you can trust my heart this is priceless, stop denying it no more fighting it, come to me, allow me to **Erase Your Pain** *for good, I will show you a love so powerful that you will never be the same, so strong to where you will never have any complaints, this is not fiction or fake I will love you for the rest of my days.*

One Special Day

Today will be the day I show you love in a special way, these words you will forever say, my King the way you love me is like no other, especially when we are wrapped up in between the covers, since I have discovered your heart you have never wanted to be apart from this love we share, as I take your hand and kiss you there on your lips I feel a shift in our moods sweeping you off your feet like a broom, consuming all of you, ready I am to give you all of me on this **One Special Day**, this love our love will never be replaced from the look upon your face I can tell my love won't ever be erased as I go low between your waist to give you a taste of my love, a special delivery sent from heaven above I will be all the drug you need, stripping off your skirt keeping the heels on your feet, my hands begin to creep up your thighs making your passion come alive spreading you wide so I can play with your pearl with my tongue, licking you slowly, welcome to my royal show as I coast through your palace, this day you have imagined so many times before after this **One Special Day** you will be forever mine to explore when in need, indeed you can come see me when you want to be pleased I continue to tease making you weak screaming out you're getting the best of me as I come up from my knees dropping my pants to the floor so I can show you how much I adore your body, climbing on top so I can pull inside it moving with a steady coast kissing you slow on your neck I haven't given you the best yet, there's more to come as you begin to cum once I penetrate deep into your atmosphere, baby have no fear for now your King is always here, I will hold you near close to my heart, never will we part for today is **One Special Day**, taking you far all you can say is I love you and the way you move inside my feelings you are rising high towards the sky to the clouds making you cry, making you rain, taking away your past pain, never will you be the same after I'm done showing you why I am the one under the sun, putting love bugs in your ear as I shift gears grabbing your legs and thighs raising them high setting them on my shoulders so I can go lower, deeper into your soul behold I'm taking your heart out of the cold forever I will hold, stroke after stroke I'm evoking your love your passion your feelings going through the ceiling through the roof I am the ultimate truth when inside doing what I do, I'm so into you, literally I know you feeling me, your legs getting tight, they squeezing me, you running trying to fight what's about to happen flipping you over so I can see that back side clapping, you love my action pulling on your hair taking you there somewhere you've never been before, this is just round one I have more in store... (To be continued).

The Greatest Gift

I sit here and realize how strong I've become, with such confidence I feel that I have finally found that one, this feeling is so strong our love will forever live on, I'm so powerful when you are in my presence, the joy you bring is the most wonderful thing I can ask for, I will forever adore, exploring this passion called love, I put no one else above you are enough, all that I need you please me to the depths of my soul, I will forever hold you close and tight fighting off anyone else with all my might, you are the only one I have in my sights, these feelings I have inside are just right, like December and April, Christmas and spring, however you want to put it, I'm falling in love with my royal Queen, my heart you uplift it to the highest point, a natural high I don't need a joint or a drink, this love will never sink, staying afloat keeping my head above water, I can't wait to meet you at the altar, receiving the blessing from your father, I know we will go further than the norm, the way our love performs when intertwined, never will I come to find another of your kind, hitting that rewind button looking at my past, the others could not last, I had to move fast and dash so I wouldn't miss my soul mate, after our very first date I knew you were the truth, the words you spoke were living proof, watching the things you do since that time your acts play so vividly in my mind, sharing my world with you for the rest of my time here on this earth, my love I can't wait until you give birth to my child, to make our family is complete, what we will teach is how to live righteous with great qualities, in today's society, with you standing beside me there's nothing I can't do, I feel indestructible, going through life knowing you have my back and that I am compatible of pleasing you in ways like never before, yes I have scored **The Greatest Gift** here on this earth, you show me your worth in so many different ways, I wouldn't mind becoming your love slave, misbehaving on purpose knowing the punishment will be worth it, you are so amazing behind closed curtains, but that's a different story for another time, right now I'm stuck on how I came to find you, a needle in a haystack, your love knocks me clear off my feet, flat on my back, never will I go backwards moving forward with you **The Greatest Gift**, my love will never shift, my heart is at a steady pace with no skips not missing a beat since you came into my life, forever you will be my wife, my Queen you are my everything.

I Won't Settle

Where do we go from here? I have no fear of being without you, I have grown to be strong since you came along, I've been caught up in your web going down walking around with a frown, not happy, not satisfied, but I tried for years upon years and it's time I move on and go forward, deserving so much more I do, the devil lives inside of you and it took me awhile to realize that you are not the one I'm supposed to spend the rest of my life with, I gave you my heart which was my gift, you had my mind in a twist wrapped around your finger, I used to linger on every word on every move coming from you, doing what I was supposed to do in this relationship, I thought I saw a life with you by my side, but all I can see is hurt and pain, it's a shame how you made my eyes rain with dark clouds above my head every day, will the sun ever shine on me, will I ever be happy, will I ever find my rose, someone who really compliments me, see I need one who will not just love me some of the time, but all the time through thick and thin, over and over again times ten, my bags are packed and I'm ready for traveling, I need a real woman not one who pretends, no more living in sin a wife who will hold me down until the end, I'm setting my standards high, I won't just settle for an extravagate night, I need one who will love me just right, for the rest of my life God I ask you to send me my wife.

My Love Divine

*I can never be the lover you want me to be, I can't give you my heart for it doesn't belong to me, I gave it away sometime way back when, from that day forth I was bound to never love again, when I kiss your lips I'm thinking of her lips, kissing her in my mind thinking of **My Love Divine**, when I said I missed you, it was she I was missing, my sweet tender to her I surrender, when making love to you I remember the things she would do putting me in a royal groove, I know you don't want to lose me and I'm sorry, but it is she who has my heart even though we are so far apart like lost art, please my love don't tell me you love me for it will be a waste of your time, reason why is because you cannot take the place of **My Love Divine** who has all my love, for now we are just living in the moment I'm just being honest, take it or leave it, but believe it when I say if she was to call me today I will drop everything and go to her, my love defers to her beck and call, I keep you near so I won't have withdrawals, once again I am sorry and all, but her love lays down the law for me, I know you can see a life between us and I'm sure it will be a plus, but it won't be right until my heart is completely over **My Love Divine**, it may take some time, hopefully you can do some things that can keep my mind off this love I once knew if you are the truth then show me the proof, no I'm not taking about sex, that's too easy, show me it's you I will be needing.*

Secret Stories Untold

Look deep into my eyes and I'll reveal my soul, scared and confused, full of **Secret Stories Untold**, a whole lifetime story will unfold, afraid to open my heart and let you find what has my feelings so bound and tied, afraid of what you may come to find knowing what's going on inside this heart of mine, allowing you to know the real me, a timid past so dismal and bleak I wouldn't want you to think that I am weak for my past made me who I am today, please tell me that forever you will stay after you hear what I have to say, I'm so scared of my heart that will not heal, I just want to be numb unable to feel, my cries for help falls on deaf ears I drown myself inside of my fears, holding back all my tears, for years I have had to deal with this hurt with this pain, are you the one who will come into my life an erase this memory from my brain, let me explain, many years ago I was hurt by someone who I thought had my best interest at heart, not knowing that person was tearing me apart from the inside out without a doubt I was blind and could not find my way to heaven, stuck in time, lost in a world that was not my own, I couldn't call anyone by phone, I couldn't run home I was all alone, no one knew what I was going through, not my family nor my crew, these words I speak are true I was caught up, trapped, I didn't know where I was going I didn't know where I was, I was just living day to day like nothing was happening, until one day I took action, I broke down and said enough is enough, dropping to my knees asking God to make me strong to make me tough, free me from this pain cast your angels around me and let them remain in my presence, if it wasn't for heaven I may still be stuck with these **Secret Stories Untold**, behold now that I am grown I can see what happened to me was in God's plan to make me a better man today, so I forgive my past for the hurt, it does not linger in my heart anymore, it's time I even the score with forgiveness, you are my witness I'm letting go of my past so that my days on this earth will outlast the stress, the hurt and pain I had buried deep down in my soul, I'm telling you this because I'm ready to let go, I am born again without sin forgiving the sin that was brought upon me, look in my eyes and you will see a new me, the devil tried, but God made me strong no longer am I weak, for now it's love I seek tell me it's you forever that will be at my side becoming my bride now that you know about my life's past. I want us to outlast our last, moving slow not fast taking my time so you know you came to find a real man in this land of earth forever I will show you my worth, holding no more **Secret Stories Untold**, in your hands my heart you will forever hold.

I Will Make You Fall in Love

With the things I can do, I will show and prove to you that love is real, with just one touch you will learn how to feel again, **I Will Make You Fall in Love** with not only what I can do in between the sheets, the way my heart screams out will make you weak, turning you into a fiend let me explain what I mean, allow me to run down this list, with just one kiss to your lips I will put you in a twist, holding you tight like a balled fist, no part of your body will be missed with my tongue making you hotter than the sun, showing you why I am the one they call King, giving you everything, yes I am your dream come true, as your voice begins to sing these words as I move through and through your body, where have you been all my life, you have broken down my walls and I'm ready to become your wife, replying is that right, shifting gears so that you can feel all my might, shining with the brightest of light, showing you that love is more than just a word, it's the acts that would make you defer to my heart, kissing on your curves playing the part, giving you everything you deserve putting my words into play so that forever you will stay, so that forever you will say I am yours, falling in love you are as I take you far holding you near, even when I am not here you can close your eyes and I will appear, taking away any fear that you may have, showing you why I will outlast your past, for I am the one who was design to fulfill your every need, wants and desires, in my heart I hold the power to love you like no other, you will be thanking my father and mother for bringing me into this world, created just for you my special girl, my beautiful woman, turning your heart hot from being cold like a kitchen oven, I will never put no one else above it, above you I will do nothing, but adore the very ground that you walk on, for so long you have waited, being patient for a King like me, my Queen I will succeed your every need, I am here for you to please, I don't mind dropping down to my knees to go in between your palace to give you more than you can ever imagine, taking your passion to a higher level once I begin to dig with my shovel, going deep where no sun can creep, I told you **I Will Make You Fall in Love** with me, this is just the start, precious you are, never will we part, for we are joined at the hip, I'm showing you that I am blessed, well endowed and fully equipped with what's between my hips as I dip into your passion of love, making you fly as high as a beautiful dove, bringing your heart from out of that cave, releasing you from the shackles no more being a slave, protecting the heart you have given to me, forever I will keep in a safe place, God has blessed the day we found each other, making you blossom like a flower in the spring time with my actions, guaranteed satisfaction, you will never come to find another love as deep as mine.

Until You Climax

Slow strokes so I can invoke your passion with all my back and forth action, satisfaction lasting until the next time we meet, I can't wait to climb in the sheets to move up your thighs with my lips taking you on an everlasting trip when my baseline hits you, cruising through your system, interlocking our hands, our hearts pumping to each other rhythm as I take your mind on this unforgettable mission, you will be hoping and wishing we never part, stroke after stroke deep into your palace I go, but let me back up and take it slow, pulling out so my tongue can go below, kissing you on your inner thighs with your head tilted back and eyes to the ceiling ready you are to enjoy this sexual healing, remember these words I'm not finished until you're finished, teasing your pearl tongue while I hold your legs up in that V-shape in due time you will feel your body begin to quake start to shake as I make my move spreading your lips to put you in a groove with my tongue pushing inside of you, licking all around your palace while sucking on you nice and slow, giving you an unbelievable show taking you to an unprecedented level as I rock your boat, your waves have my bed soaked pushing your legs further towards your chin so I can go deeper within, tonight you will win, my tongue is a pen writing in cursive signing my name all over your body, excited you are ready to explode like a shooting star, can you image what I'm about to do next, I've been rated the best lover of the year, *locking your thighs with my arms to pull you near close to me, my feet are steady and firm on the floor taking you to the corner of the bed so that I can perform my undying strokes, get ready to let go as I float through your palace to empower you with a love sent from heaven above my sexy lady are you ready to feel my real deal, pulling in slow so that you feel every inch of my royal taking my time I don't want to spoil this moment with busting early, damn you are worthy of my actions taking all this satisfaction, switching positions ready I am to climb all the way on top putting your legs on my shoulders so that I can get into my pushup position, with your hands on my hips these words rolls from your lips baby go slow you're so big I need you to coast until I can take your stroke, slow I go making you float high above doing you just right, my love is outta this world, your nails are piercing deep with your legs wrapped around me I feel you getting weak as I fill your cup with more than enough, I begin to hit it hard do you rough, making you scream and shout showing you what I'm about, remember what I said I'm not finished* **Until You Climax**, *pushing in and out, taking you to the limit as you climax biting me on my shoulder leaving love marks, you're shooting like darks, you can't stop climaxing, your body's going limp and relaxing, as a smile comes upon your face, saying to me satisfaction.*

You Have Awakened My Love that Lives Inside of Me

My love what have you done to me, you have my eyes wide open, it's you I only see, forever your love I will seek, just You and Me are on my mind, our hearts have become intertwined, bonded tight never to come unwound, how did I ever come to find you my true love, beautiful you are, my heart not even putting up a fight allowing you to just walk right in, ready to marry you so we don't live in sin, this love will never come to an end, holding you close within, deep down to my soul, **You have Awakened My Love** that was buried with the rest of my Secrets Untold, say that you will never let go of my heart, tell me that we will never part, you have found me like lost art, dug deep into my hidden treasure I already can see that your love cannot be measured, you bring me so much pleasure with just your conversation, stimulating my mind, In due Time I will put that arch in your spine, showing you a real love for the first time in your life and vice versa, my tongue writes in cursive when I go to work between your margins, can you hear my heart calling out for your love, you are my angel sent by the man himself above, I prayed for a Queen, a beautiful dove, you just don't know what you have done, Awakening a sleeping giant, defining the meaning of love through the love you give, wrapped around your finger I am in a twist, our first kiss will be explosive, no part of your body will go missed, with each touch our hearts will grow closer, *fulfilling all your secret fantasy, making sure no need of yours will go unturned, this love our love was meant, I yearn for your touch, your kiss your lips just put me in a groove that I don't ever want to lose, your smile can move mountains, in between the sheets I will have you overflowing dripping wet like a leaking faucet, showing you why I am boss, calling me King in that sweet tone of yours, this love will never be lost, my love can only be bought with the purity of your heart, so please tell me again that we will never be apart, baby tell me you will always hold my heart tightly, close to yours, I feel so much joy now that you are in my life,* **You Have Awakened My Love that Lives Inside of Me**, *I didn't know anyone was able to dig that deep, but you came and showed me that all things are possible, making me believe again, with you by my side I can't lose, win is all I will do with you doing the things you do, once I enter your palace with my royal staff we will become stuck like glue, I had no clue that you will come into my world and show me a real woman, not some little girl spinning me in circles and twirls, you are special and I know what I have in my hands, already making plans I am for the future, I'm not fronting so it's me you better get used to, this is a lifetime commitment, I feel no resentment, tempted I am to get down on bended knee, do you see what you have done,* **You Have Awakened My Love that Lives Inside of Me**, *all I see is You and me, forever we will be by each other's side, every night holding you close and tight, never letting go with all my might giving* you a Royal Show, when I touch you low there's no limits when I go and go, taking you higher to another level, stronger than any drug I am, becoming my fiend you are my shining star, this love will go far and beyond you are my number one under the sun, looking no further, because I have discovered a love like no other, could this really be happening, satisfaction finally, showing you that I'm all you will ever need, falling in love you will be with what I can do in between the sheets, the words you speak makes me weak, forever you and me are on repeat in my head, in your bed is where I want to be, with you wrapped up in my arms, no more worries baby no need to be alarmed I will always keep you warm and safe until my dying day, this love will never be erased, you can see the sincerity upon my face, these words I will always say, I love you for who you are, **You Have Awakened My Love** once again, covering up my scars, what a beautiful woman you are, the luckiest man on earth I am, I can't say it enough, like a volcano my love is about to erupt, overflowing with happiness and joy, just You and Me on this forever voyage, on this forever quest, we will get through any test life throws our way, my love is here to stay.

I Can't Sleep Without You

Laying here in complete darkness, trying to fall asleep, but when my eyes are closed all I can see is you, my thoughts begin to race, wishing you were by my side in my arms on this lonely night, I can visualize it now the things I will be doing, first I will tell you how much I am in love you with, then I will act on the passion I hold inside of my heart for you, showing you the greatest me, the greatest love all night long, showing you why your love stays constantly on my mind, making your love walls come down with what I have in store, reassured that you will deeply appreciate my skills, giving you love at will, at your beckoning call, my love I have fallen for you, wishing I was next to you, so that I can kiss you soft and slowly, with our tongues twisting as my hands move below your waist into that special place, holding you tightly even in darkness you shine with the brightest of light, giving you the best love that you ever had, my sleep tonight I fight needing you by my side so I can get through this lonely night, can you feel my plight, I want to feel your lips all through the night, everywhere and between can you feel what I mean, I hope you are at home thinking the same thing, baby your love is so good I have to break it down like, boom, clap, boom, boom, clap, boom, clap, clap, boom, clap, deep inside of you is where I want to be, with your nails putting scratches on my back as I attack your love with my passionate strokes, empowering you with this love as I coast through your walls, through your secret garden, freaking you with the way I'm pushing inside of your cave, damn I wish you were here, ready I am to misbehave, turning into your Love Slave, with just One Night I made your heart all mine, all it took was that one time assuring you that you could never come to find another guy of my kind, these words you spoke last time I was deep into your spine, oh my what have you done tell me, say you will forever stay in my life without thinking twice each and every time I will do your body Just Right, I need your body here with me every night my love, lost I am without my dove in my arms, all I want to do is perform these love acts I have hidden inside, if only you were here tonight, I won't be laying here up all night going out my mind, staring at the time, past two I don't even know what to do, every time I close my eyes I see no one but you, tell me what am I to do, when **I Can't Sleep Without You.**

For Eternity

When I look upon your face, when I think about how I feel when blessed with your grace, you may not know this, but you take my breath away, with really no words that can describe how I feel inside, sometimes I break down and cry tears of joy when I think about your love I have come to explore, with each day that passes I adore your more and more, you're nothing like the norm, the way you perform these passion acts, tells my heart that it is you where I want to be, through my eyes you can see my love raising high flying through the sky I am with no complaints, I thank you for entering my life and bringing love to my soul, this love I can't control, never will I let go, **For Eternity** I can watch your love magic show, the way you move slowly when on top hitting the right spot, taking the temperature in the room from cold to being hot, you have just what I want, regretting my choice I don't, you are who I need by my side sent here to please me all through the night, with the way you kiss my lips and the way you sway your hips as you dip and slide down **My Rollercoaster Ride**, from the look in your eyes and the moans that are coming from deep down inside I can feel that I take you just as high as you take me, it's us **For Eternity**, what we do in the sheets is just a sneak peek to how I'm going to love you for the rest of our natural days, listen to what I say, with each passing day I will come up with a new way to show you love, my angel, my dove, there's no limit I can't reach when I think about the love you give to me, I become strong not weak, your love lives within me, our heartbeat is in tune with one another I have discovered love for the first time, blowing my mind you are taking me to new heights, I knew this was right from that very first sight of you, shining brighter than the sun you were, claiming you I was, calling you the one without knowing your name, it's obvious you felt the same, my leading lady, my beautiful dame, after that day I've never been the same, you take the cake, I can't wait no longer, on bended knee I am, not playing no games, listen to what I'm saying, I love you and will continue to love you until my eyes close for good, my love for you is tough as nails, thick as wood, I am here to stay, no one can take your love away from me, you are my Queen, my everything under the star light skies, please say yes you will be my bride, you have me open, my feelings cannot hide, your heart is mine, I belong to you and you belong to me, you are where I want to be **For Eternity**.

If I...

If I *were to take you by the hand and lead you to my Lovers' Land would you comply with what I want to do to you, will you allow me to take you on a never-ending ride, for just One Night, allow me to make you feel Just Right, I want you to feel alive again, with me there's no end, you will cum again, again and again and even once more before you leave my room and close the door,* ***If I*** *pulled you close to hold you tight you will feel that I won't ever let go gazing into your eyes before I start to kiss you slowly you will begin to float on cloud nine, as I unwind your body taking my time before I go inside your palace, making you feel like a woman should, the other guys had you misunderstood, only If I could just show you what it feels like to be loved by a real man, a King, I want to show you what I mean,* ***If I*** *pick you up by your thighs to lay you down before I go inside massaging your body with my hands then my tongue, let me show why I am number one when it comes to this love making your body will be yearning and aching for my love long after I'm done, starting from the top of your head with a kiss to your frontal lobe as I sit up to pull off your shirt to see your lovely body exposed, working my way down past your thighs pulling off the heels to see those pretty toes, almost you are fully exposed, only your pants are left to go, as I pull them down slow, enjoying my show you are, it's time you get treated like the special woman you are, I'm about to take you far,* ***If I*** *start to slide my hands up* your thighs before I come inside your passion will begin to rise, tonight you will be loved Just Right, looking deep into your eyes I see that I'm stimulating your mind as well as your body, before I pull inside it I want you to know that I am in control, I want you to lay back relax and just let go, baby enjoy this Royal Show that I am about to put on, I'm about to have you raining like a storm, **If I** perform these acts you will come running back wanting me to attack your every desire, calling me sire, King **If I** go in between with my tongue teasing your breasts as I caress your pearl with my index finger, you're becoming an R&B singer hitting notes as I coast from your breasts past your waist to give you a taste of what I have in store, ready I am to explore your secret pleasure, nine and a half yes I've been measured can you handle what's between my hips, **If I** begin to slip and slide through your tunnel gripping your thighs they become tight as I pull inside going slow before I hit you with all my might, my love game is outta this world, outta sight, If you can handle what I pitch tonight then I just might invite you back for another night, pinning your hands to the bed so there won't be no scratching no fight, no running as I bless you tonight, are you ready for my **If I**, will you comply with what I want to do next, this is the greatest love you've ever felt, as I dwell inside your walls I stand tall to give you all of me, wrapping your legs around my waist staring deep into your face as I take my rightful place, these words you will say, baby be careful with what you're about to do, you're making me bust all over you with the things you're doing, never leave me my love I will be ruined, smiling I am because I told you **If I** take you there you wouldn't want to go anywhere, lifting you high in the air, pressing you against the wall no worry baby I have strength in these arms and legs you won't fall, the only thing that will be coming down is your waterfall, going deep in all kissing you on your neck you're kissing on my cheeks, weak you are, shooting passion like a blazing star, pushing your limits taking you further than ever before, I told you I'm nothing like the norm once I start to perform with my **If I** all night I will have your love flying high, it's no joke it's no lie with what I can do with my **If I** giving you The Greatest Gift from above making you rain and rain as I swim through your walls erasing any pain you may have, from your screams and moans I can tell that you are glad you didn't pass on my **If I**, alive you are as I put you down to turn you around for the grand finale, with your legs spread apart I kiss you soft before I pull into your nice, wet and warm dark palace, you never thought or even image the passion that was going to be laid down here tonight as I begin to finish this course of love, giving it to you hard and rough, my **If I** you can't get enough pulling on your hair squeezing on your butt as we both erupt, erupt, erupt with passion and love feeling the air, no way this night can ever be compared, as we lay here to reminisce on what just happened, you stand up clapping giving me that standing ovation, loving our sensational love affair, with thoughts of I could never compare this King to the rest you must attest, that I am the best you ever had, cradled in my arms, saying that you are glad at what we have, your **If I** is amazing my palace is still blazing as we sleep the night away, in thoughts you want nothing more than to forever stay in my Kingdom, to forever stay by my side in love you are with my **If I**.

My Heart and Soul

My love it's you I belong to, my love is living proof that I want no one, but you, these words are true, I can't express my feelings enough, when the going gets tough you are here to uplift my head up high, letting me know things will be alright, see it's not the worldly possessions that keep you by my side, it's the love you know that I hold inside, through my brown eyes you can see how my soul shines when your near, with you I have no fear, my heart won't allow any other woman to come near or even close, your love makes me shout and boast, pouring you a glass of wine so I can make a toast to the love that we share, suspended in the air, note that I can't compare, never will I dare to leave your heart, never will we grow apart, with each passing second, minute, hour, days, weeks, months and years you remove my doubts and fears, you're **My Heart and Soul**, can't you see the way this aura glows around me, especially when I kiss your lips my heart begins to do flips, igniting my soul taking me on this lifetime trip the way you move those hips puts me in a love groove called you, singing your song forever you and me will always be together, getting through and stormy weather, all I can do is think of you when we are apart, I can't get you off my mind, your beautiful smile stops me in my tracks, pausing the time, making me forget what I was doing at the moment, tell me it's me that you are wanting for the rest of your life, I don't think twice when it comes to loving you, I do what I can to show and prove that I am worthy enough to have you by my side, oh baby the way you make my passion rise brings tears to my eyes, yes sometimes I do cry when thinking about how much love I have stored inside of this **Heart and Soul** of mine, you are the key to my happiness, bless the day you came my way and showed me what the word love really means, searching and searching for you my Queen, in you I have found exactly what I need, you fulfill my every desire, setting my soul on fire, easing the pain that once lives inside my heart, lost I was like the Sparta treasure at sea, you came and rescue you me, the same old me I will never be, why because I have you my beautiful Queen, can you feel what I mean, note this is not lust, but the love we make is real you can trust that **My Heart and Soul** will never fail you, keeping it real with you is what I will always do, I'm nothing like your past, what you see right here before you is no hidden mask, I can handle any task thrown my way, sharing my world with you so that forever you will stay, showing you brighter days with no dark clouds above your head, promise I do to always be here for you, there's no one else, but you I need in my life, wrapped up in your paradise, my mind doesn't think twice, never will we go cold, forever I will hold your love close to **My Heart and Soul.**

One of a Kind

They call me King because of the way I will make you fiend with the way I please once I go in between you will feel what I mean, never will you come to find another man like me because I am **One of a Kind***, sending chills through your body up your spine, all it takes is just one time for you to fall in love with this* **One of a Kind***, stroking you up and down making you change faces, taking my time, hitting you with my love that is so divine, making you want me really bad since the first time you had a piece of this* **One of a Kind***, traveling through your mind all through the day and night hoping I come through and hit you with all my strength and might, the way I do your body nice and slow, kissing you from head to toe, going in making you float high with this power I hold inside, bringing your love walls down, having your heart wide open, wishing and hoping I take you away from those clowns you been around, look at what you have found, hitting my phone telling me you laying around in nothing, but your bra and panties, wanting me to come home so we can get it on, smiling happy that I am on my way entering your door so I can feel your space up with my well-endowed, soon I will be enjoying the sounds you make and the words you will say once I take my rightful place, but first let me set the mood, lighting a few candles and turning on some slow jams to really put you in a groove, with the way I'm about to move deep inside your palace will make you feel like I'm* doing magic, but this no illusion the way our bodies are fusing, kissing you while my hands are moving up your thighs to your pleasant surprise, coming alive I am standing bulging through my pants ready to start this dance, my **One of a Kind** is ready to be placed in your hands, as you sit down on the edge of the bed to unbuckle my pants, sliding them to the floor ready you are to explore my love with your tongue and jaws, your neighbors may call the law before we are done, tonight will be hotter than a summer day, beaming like the sun, holding me close so I won't run doing things with your tongue have me in awe, the way you're working your mouth and jaws has me going insane I see you're not playing no games with my **One of a Kind**, tick tock, tick tock we not worried about the time, going all night is fine by me, changing positions so I can give you a taste of me, pushing you back so I can attack your pleasure, you're about to rain like a thunder storm, with the way my tongue is about to perform, ready, set go from your head to your toes, check my flow as I give you a Royal Show, first I start off slow kissing your neck with a lick here and a lick there, making your feelings come alive, now you are aware that I'm about to take you there, rubbing on your lovely breasts yes I caress your nipples with the tip of my tongue making you feel that freaky sensation, giving you a mix of my compilation, loving the love faces you're making, before I go all in and start to swim through your pool palace I want you to set back and just relax as I slide down your waistline, my *right and left hands spread your thighs wide so I can feel you deep inside, my tongue is about to take you for a ride, signing my name on it, crossing my t's as I lick in between your thighs making you cum sooner than you thought, splashing and dashing through your walls of love, taking you higher and above, digging deep as I suck you soft, lost you were, found by the one and only King here on this earth, showing you your worth as you start to go berserk, you giving me that sticky face loving your taste I am, pushing your legs towards your chin so I can go deeper within, my tongue has become a pin writing all over your body ready I am to pull inside your pleasure P, with my Royal D, like a missile I'm locked and loaded seeking your love entering your cave making you feel what it is you have been missing, loving you like I never loved nobody else, kissing you softly and sweetly as I go deep in giving you The Greatest Gift, no spot will be missed as I do circles and twist inside of it, loving this rhythm I'm putting on you, with the way I groove you never want to lose my* **One of a Kind**, *always and forever I will stay on your mind, fitting tight like a glove my beautiful dove, I continue to take you higher and above, stroke after stroke my power invokes your soul, you begin to lose control, your legs start to shake, you scream out I can't take it, but don't stop with what you're doing on top, you're hitting my special spot, cumin' again, as I pull out to spin you around placing you in front of the mirror so that I can see those love faces you make while I break* you down from behind, loving your moans and cries, pushing slowly inside making sure you feel all my love divine through and through your spine with that sexy arch in your back, under locking my arms through your shoulders so you feel me deep as I attack with my long strokes, coasting slow before I pick up my coast, floating in and out, without a doubt satisfaction is written all over your face with what I'm doing in between your waist, you start to run, but I'm on the chase turning you around wrapping your legs around my waist so I can pick you up to give you that finale eruption, tomorrow I will be at the top of your discussion with your girlfriends, we're almost to the end as I slide back in to lift you high for the last time as I rip through your spine running my fingers through your hair driving you crazy insane, skipping work you will be, giving you my overtime with no complaints from you as I do what I do, bouncing you back and forth, going north and south with my **One of a Kind**, cumin' together we are at the same time, my love will forever stay on your mind, as I bed you goodnight you will never come to find another **One of a Kind** in this life.

The Love of My Life

The very first time I laid my eyes upon your beautiful face, I knew it was you **The Love of my Life***, from that very day I knew it was you finally my wife come true, in my heart you will always stay, I used to dream of you my Queen, each time I shut my eyes I saw you in my sights running through my mind, consuming all my thoughts and time my beautiful find, grateful I am that you brought your love to my life,* **The Love of my Life***, you are by far the only woman I will ever need, succeeding all my expectations, stimulating my eternal soul, tide and bound by your love never do I ever want to be let go, you have exposed my true feelings giving me sexual healing, erasing my pain that once lived deep inside my Heart and Soul, forever I want you to hold my love close to your heart, no one or nothing will be able to tear us apart, caught and tangled up in your web I am, continue to feed me your love, my love sent from the pearly gates of heaven my lucky number seven, since I was eleven I knew I wanted a love so true and dear, feared I did to end up settling for something that is not worthy of my love, my God has sent you to me created from My Rib to give me pleasure in so many different ways, taking me to new heights and above, in return I will show you that real love really does exist and I will never misbehave or trade you for another, granting your every wish, I want you to become the mother of my child, I'm going crazy, going wild inside and out without a doubt I will climb to* the highest mountain to scream and shout, professing how much I am in love with you my Queen, you bring me so much joy that lives in the inside of my heart, I smile when I think of you when we are apart, knowing that soon we will be back into each other arms, I love our love acts that we perform when you're kissing me softly with those kissable lips, my world begins to do flips once I take a dip into those hips of yours, oh how I love to explore your passion, enjoy I do all our tongue lashing, our back and forth action brings me more than satisfaction, it takes me to a place where I never been before, my love it's you and only you that I will adore for the rest of my life, you are **The Love of My Life**, I can't stress it enough, but never will I think twice when it comes to your heart, with you by my side I will continue to go far and beyond, you show me show much care, I'm so fond of you always I want you here, near and close, forever you and me- **The Love of My Life**.

Her Empty Space

*Tired I am of seeing your eyes running down like waterfalls, it's getting to the point where I'm ready to come and grab you, take you away from there, allow me to be your air so that you can breathe again, your heart and pain I can erase, I can see your **Empty Space** through the look you give upon your face, each and every time you come my way your heart is at a race, I want you to let me come inside and set your love at a steady pace, allow me to take you to another place, away from the frowns and all the put downs, uplifting you high I will, building you up taking you higher than the tallest hills here on this earth, once again I know your worth, take my hand my love, I want to show you a love like never before, you should be cherished and adored, never should you be broken down to the floor, today is a new day, I am here to stay in your life to give you what you want, becoming your husband you my wife, my Queen yes I am your King, I want you sitting right next to me on my throne is where you belong, I welcome you with open arms, showing you something new I will, check my skills, it's all about you, sit back and relax as I rub your pretty little feet, I finally get to see your smile that comes across your cheeks, with me you will never be weak, well only when we are in between the sheets and I'm giving you all of me, what's that you say, you want me to show you and give you a taste, thirsty for you I am like an alcoholic at a bar, what I'm about to do will have you going far,* further than ever before, no more of you not getting yours, as I take my time slithering up your thighs from your feet, kissing you slowly with a lick to your inner thighs, I see and feel that your passion is for once in life about to come alive, this right here will be a lifetime ride, filling your **Empty Space** so that forever you will never feel anymore hurt or pain, never will you be the same, with the love I give, you will never have any complaints, God has blessed the day I came and took you away from that clown who had no clue of what he had in the palm of his hands, no more being sad, your heart can smile and dance For Eternity, forever you and me as I continue to creep past your thighs up your waist line kissing on your stomach, humming to the tune of your body my love you are going to feel so different once I hit you with my If I, deep pushing inside our love will rise to the top floor in this Trump Tower, your soul and heart I'm ready to conquer and devour, the clock is passing another hour, beautiful you are my wild flower, my rose, moving up your breasts, I am getting close to fully exposing your true feelings, with just one touch of my lips to your lips you will feel what you have missed, hitting your spot with a lick to your neck, you haven't felt nothing yet, tonight I'm going to make you sweat like never before, I want you to know that I am all yours, as I explore your inner love, I come up to kiss your lips our tongues begin to twist with my hands wrapped around your hips going round and round in circles we are, blazing like a shooting star, making you feel like a real woman should, I would do what's needed to be done to show you that you are the one, no more second guessing yourself, what I'm going to do is restore your confidence, you are heaven sent and you should never forget that as I begin my attack, showing you more love with just the kisses I'm giving, taking you high and above the clouds past the skies, my love will never cease it will never lie, this passion will forever stay alive, even when I am not at your side you will be able to close your eyes and feel me deep inside, here I go as I go back where I started to give you a Royal show, down below spreading you wide so that I can come inside with my tongue filling your **Empty Space**, now you can feel where I coming from, your body becomes tight your legs are going numb, tensing up, you're about to cum, giving you that green light, go, go, go your juices flowing more and more than ever before, with my knees on the floor and your hands rubbing my head, tonight you will be fed with greatest love known to man, as I stand to give you what you have been patiently waiting for, no I am not done exploring your **Empty Space**, taking you outta space with my flying rocket going through and through hitting your special pocket, rocking back and forth in and out, as you scratch and shout loud from your mouth, there's no doubt about the grooves I have in store for you, loving everything I do, putting you in a mood you never what to lose, remembering this time for the rest of your life as I go deeper into your spine, massaging your palace with my royal, what you imagine is just right, you knew once I touched I will have your heart for life, blessing you I am all through the night, taking my time, letting you know that you will never come to find another of my kind, not in this lifetime, making you believe in trust once again, with me you will forever win, you're already making plans to always be a part of my world with the way my love acts have you caught up in a twirl, erupting you are, forever my girl my beautiful find, I'm will make sure your **Empty Space** will be forever filled with this love of mine, this is God's will, He put me in your life to show you what love is really about, to show you what it really means to have true and honest love, yes I was sent from heaven above my angel, always we will be tangled in each other hearts, never will you ever be lost again, for as long as I live I will give you the utmost love that there is to give, going deeper into your ribs when I fold your legs back to give you my encore, forever yours, my heart belongs to you, there's nothing I won't do, my heart is plain right here on the table, I know that I am able to fulfill your every desire, taking you out of that fire you were once in, as I go in marrying you I will so we don't live in sin, never will this love come to an end, forever I will fill **Her Empty Space**.

Dontae Cottrell

About the Author

Dontae Cottrell grew up in Compton, CA, facing different trials and tribulations, making it through by the grace of God. With a college education, becoming an author was not in his plans. He had his sights on making it to the NBA, as basketball was his life. It wasn't until the summer of 2003 when he began to put his feelings to paper, he realized that words and poetry became second nature. His mind is so vivid that it's hard to tell reality and fantasy apart. As you journey through his mind, you will come to find a stand up guy who is kind at heart. It took him a while to find his niche and at twenty-nine years of age, he feels he has finally arrived. He is ready for the world. This book is only the beginning.

www.ingramcontent.com/pod-product-compliance
Lightning Source LLC
Chambersburg PA
CBHW050556170426
43201CB00011B/1709